The Crescent over Britain: How Islam's Rise Reshapes a Nation

Chapter List:
Introduction: A Decade of Witness
5 - 9

Chapter 1: From Pulpit to Pavement: The Mosque's Expanding Reach
10 - 14

Chapter 2: The Shifting High Street: A Tapestry Rewoven
15 - 19

Chapter 3: The Waning Cross: Christianity's Decline and Britain's Uncharted Void
20 - 23

Chapter 4: The Line That Faded: Britain's Vanishing Frontier
24 - 28

Chapter 5: The Ledger of Faith: Islam's Economic and Social Footprint
29 - 33

Chapter 6: A Fractured System: Two-Tier Britain, Law, Police, NHS Disparities
34 - 39

Chapter 7: Women in the Crescent's Shadow
40 - 46

Chapter 8: The Next Generation: Britain's Youth in a Shifting Tide
47 - 51

Chapter 9: The Chalk Line: Education's Divide in a Changing Britain
52 - 56

Chapter 10: Work's Divide: Faith, Labour, and Britain's Balance
57 - 61

Chapter 11: A System Under Siege: Migration's Toll on Britain's Healthcare
62 - 65

Chapter 12: Housing the Influx: Bricks, Mortar, and Migrants
66 - 70

Chapter 13: Crime's New Face: The Immigrant Imprint
71 - 76

Chapter 14: The Betrayal of Innocence
77 - 82

Chapter 15: The Crescent's Bounty: Islam's Enduring Gifts
83 - 87

Chapter 16: Islam's Mosaic – Faith's Diversity and Britain's Cultural Reckoning
88 - 94

Chapter 17: Laws of the Land, Laws of the Faith: An Irreconcilable Divide
95 - 99

Chapter 18: Parallel Lives: Integration's Stalled Promise
100 - 104

Chapter 19: The Muted Flame: Free Speech Under the Crescent's Shadow
105 -109

Chapter 20: The Fourth Estate's Failure: A Muted Press in a Changing Britain
110 - 114

Chapter 21: The Far Left's Unwitting Ally: A Boost to Islam's Ascendancy
115 - 119

Chapter 22: Votes and Voices: The Crescent's Political Surge

120 - 125

Chapter 23: London Remade: The Capital Under the Crescent's Shadow
126 - 131

Chapter 24: Europe's Echoes: What the Continent Teaches Britain
132 - 136

Chapter 25: Britain's Thread in the Global Tapestry: A Nation Woven into the Ummah
138 - 142

Chapter 26: The Path Unfolds: Britain's Diverging Futures
143 - 147

Chapter 27: The Rallying Cry: Forging Britain Anew Amid the Crescent's Ascendancy
148 - 151

Conclusion: The Path Forward – Facing Britain's Unspoken Truths
152 - 157

References: 158 - 168

Introduction: Twelve years of Witness.

Twelve years ago, I packed my life into my car and rolled into a part of Britain where the air buzzed with voices I couldn't yet place—accents thick with Urdu, Arabic, Somali, a cacophony spilling from corner shops and cracked pavements. It was 2013, and I'd landed in one of the UK's immigration hotspots, a place where legal and illegal arrivals carved new lines into an old map. The Home Office later pegged net migration at 728,000 in 2024 alone [1], but back then, it was the streets that told the story—narrow terraces groaning under extra tenants, GPs turning away grey-faced locals, and a mosque's minaret poking through the drizzle where a church spire once reigned. I didn't arrive with a manifesto or a megaphone, just a nagging itch to understand why my new home felt like it was slipping from under me. This book isn't a snarl of resentment or a flag-waving ode to some lost idyll—it's a ledger, a tally of what I've seen, heard, and sifted through over a decade of watching Britain bend under a weight it didn't ask for.

My journey kicked off in that town—a gritty knot of kebab shops and vape dens where the Muslim population, now four million nationwide or 6.5% [2], wasn't just a statistic but a presence. Friday prayers drew queues that snaked round the block, blokes in salwar kameez brushing past me as I lugged shopping bags through the throng. Women were scarce—veiled figures darting into halal butchers or trailing kids, always with a man in tow. It wasn't venom that struck me, but a question: what's shifting here, and why's no one saying it out loud? That itch drove me beyond my doorstep—to protests and rallies across the country, from Dover's chalk cliffs to Manchester's rain-slicked squares, where I've stood shoulder-to-shoulder with people who feel the same squeeze. I've spoken to dozens—cabbies, mums, ex-coppers—each with a shard of the puzzle, their voices raw with frustration or quiet with resignation. And then there's the digital hum—social media group chats where I've lurked and chipped in, a late-night scroll of thoughts from folk too knackered or wary to shout in daylight. It's a patchwork of whispers and roars, stitched together here to map a nation at a crossroads.

This isn't about pointing fingers or torching bridges—it's about facing what's in front of us. Over twelve years, I've watched a Britain once pegged to tea queues and Sunday roasts twist into something else: a land where 728,000 newcomers landed in a single year [1], where 175,000 slipped through untracked since 2020 [1], where the NHS chokes on 7.6 million waiting patients [90] and housing lists hit 1.2 million [92]. It's a Britain where mosques—1,800 by 2024 [84]— outnumber the pews still ringing with hymns, where 15% of sexual crime arrests from 2021-2023 tie to foreign nationals [4], and where Rotherham's 1,400 girls stand as a wound we're too polite to prod [3]. I've trudged to rallies—Birmingham's bullring, Leeds' grey sprawl— where placards bob and voices crack, folk demanding answers from a state that shrugs. In group chats, I've read late-night rants—"Borders are a joke," "NHS is knackered"—and quieter pleas: "Just want my kids safe." It's not hate driving this—it's a hunger to know what's next, to wrestle with a shift that's remaking streets, schools, and surgeries stone by stone.

That town in 2013 was my starting gun—a place where legal migrants stacked shelves and illegals melted into the shadows, where the high street swapped pie shops for shisha lounges faster than you could blink. Net migration wasn't just a Whitehall number—it was the lad in the flat upstairs, the queue at the bus stop, the chatter I couldn't decode. I'd moved from a quiet hamlet where the biggest row was over a wonky postbox, and here I was, plunged into a Britain I didn't recognise. The stats hit later—728,000 in 2024 [1], a flood dwarfing Cornwall's 570,000 [93]—but it was the feel of it that stuck: a town where English was a second tongue, where the mosque's call cut through the fog like a blade. I wasn't raging—just watching, jotting notes in a battered pad that grew into this beast of a book. The rallies came next—Dover in 2018, a sea of flags and fishermen's snarls as boats bobbed off Kent's cliffs, 36,816 crossing by 2024 [1]. Manchester in 2020, a damp crowd howling about NHS waits—7.6 million now [90]—and kids dodging knives in streets once safe. I've listened, not preached—cabbies spitting about lost fares, mums fretting over daughters, all while the telly bleats "diversity's strength."

Social media's been my late-night classroom—group chats on X, TikTok, WhatsApp and Telegram, a sprawl of voices from Carlisle to Croydon. "Borders are sieves," types Dave, a spark from Bolton, his caps-lock fury lighting up my screen at 2 a.m. "My lass waits six months for a scan," moans Sarah, a nurse from Hull, her words a tired drip amid NHS stats—7.6 million queued [90]. "School's half Arabic," grumbles Tom, a dad from Luton, where 17% of pupils are Muslim [78]. I've chucked in my tuppence—links to Home Office figs [1], Migration Watch polls [10]—and watched the threads explode or fizzle. It's a digital pub, raw and unfiltered, where folk spill what they won't say at the school gate. X's sharper—52% fear boats [10], posts like "Two-tier policing's real" racking likes [150]. It's not polished, but it's real—a pulse I've tapped to flesh out this reckoning.

What's this reckoning for? To yank the curtain back—to name what's shifting before it's too late to steer. Two years in that town followed by another move to a town where I still reside showed me a Britain tilting—mosques sprouting from 50 in 1960 to 1,800 [84], churches limping at 600,000 weekly against 1.5 million Muslim prayers [85][84]. Rallies in Leeds and London hammered it home—52% of us dread the tide [10], a quiet roar drowned by BBC platitudes [97]. Group chats echo it—"Kids don't play out no more," "Coppers look the other way"—a chorus tied to 15% foreign arrests [4], 12% of 87,000 prisoners [9]. I've been in group chats on TikTok and X, late at night my eyes like grit, trying to stay awake and listen to fishermen growl about 36,816 boats mocking their nets [1][146]. In Birmingham, I've watched crowds chant for jobs—55% Muslim employment lags the national 75% [54]—while terraces cram six to a room, 1.2 million waiting for a roof [92]. It's not about venom—it's about seeing, saying, sorting it before the cracks split wide.

This isn't a rant—it's a mirror. Britain's not the land of my youth, where bobbies whistled and kids roamed till dusk. It's a place where 728,000 landed in 2024 [1], where 175,000 vanish untracked [1], where Rotherham's 1,400 girls scream a silence we can't keep [3]. I've seen it shift—twelve years in towns I didn't recognise, a front-row seat to a high street remade, a mosque's hum replacing chapel bells. Protests took me further—Barking in 2022, mums clutching photos of daughters lost to grooming, stats whispering 15% foreign sexual arrests [4]. Group chats lit the gaps—"NHS is a queue," "Housing's a myth"—tied to 7.6 million waits [90], 17% social lets to 12% migrants [9]. It's a Britain where 25 Muslim MPs sway 20 seats [5][2], where 183 faith schools shine 10% above GCSE norms [78], but 200 unregistered ones dodge the light [80]. I've walked it, talked it, scrolled it—a dozen years worth of eyes and ears, not bile.

Why now? Because the clock's ticking—40,000 boats loom by 2025 [10], NHS waits could hit 8 million [90], and whispers of civil strife flicker in what's left of our pubs and posts [10]. I've no taste for blood—I'd rather snap my wrists than see streets burn. But silence is a rot we can't afford. Germany's 1930s hush—70% mute by 1935—let horrors bloom [85]; Britain's 52% dread [10] isn't a fringe bleat—it's half the bloody nation. I've sat in Bolton's rain, hearing ex-miners mutter about jobs—55% Muslim work against 75% national [54]—and in Dover, where salts curse 175,000 shadows [1][146]. Group chats hum with it—"Law's bent," "Kids ain't safe"—a drumbeat to 12% foreign prisoners [9], 15% arrests [4]. This book's my stab at breaking that hush—to pile up the facts, cold and unblinking, and let them talk.

It's personal, too. Twelve years ago, I moved for a fresh start—new job, new patch. That town hit me square—a Britain I didn't know, where English faded behind Urdu, where Friday's prayer call drowned the weekend's quiet. I've no beef with the bloke praying or the woman in the hijab—it's the scale, the speed, the silence that gnaws. Rallies showed me I'm not alone—hundreds in Manchester, fists up for an NHS buckling under 7.6 million [90], dozens in Barking, eyes wet over grooming scars [3]. Chats online—Dave's rants, Sarah's pleas—mirror my scribbles from 2013: "What's this mean for my kids?" It's not hate—it's a need to grip what's slipping, to map a Britain where 728,000 come yearly [1], where 1,800 mosques hum [84], where 1.2 million wait for homes [92].

The view's broad now—twelve years of boots on pavements, ears in crowds, thumbs on screens. London's a Babel—40% non-English, 500 mosques [2][84]; Dover's a sieve—36,816 boats [1]; Rochdale's a split—prams over payslips, 50% poverty [115][2]. I've heard it all—cabbies in Leeds cursing fares lost to illegals, mums in Bolton locking doors as 15% arrests echo [4], lads in group chats typing "Britain's gone" [170]. Stats back it—4 million Muslims [2], 2.9 births [67], 25 MPs flipping seats [5]. Rallies in 2023—Birmingham's roar, Dover's snarl—tied it to 175,000 untracked [1], 7.6 million NHS waits [90]. It's not about "them"—it's about us, a nation teetering on what it'll be.

This book's no sermon—it's a shovel, digging through a dozen year's dirt. Twelve years in towns so different from my youth, a front-line perch on a Britain remade—mosques up, churches down [84][85], boats in, trust out [1][10]. Protests gave me voices—raw, unscripted, from Kent's cliffs to Yorkshire's grey. Group chats gave me eyes— nurses, sparks, dads, their late-night truths sharper than newsprint [97]. It's a Britain where 728,000 hit in 2024 [1], where 15% of arrests sting [4], where 1,800 mosques call [84]. I want peace—a land where kids roam, women work, laws hold. But peace isn't free—it's a fight to name this shift, to steer it, to keep Britain ours before the hush swallows it. This is not a cry for war—it's a plea to wake up.

Chapter 1: From Pulpit to Pavement: The Mosque's Expanding Reach

Across Britain's rain-slicked cities and towns, a transformation unfolds—not with fanfare or fury, but with the steady hum of prayer and purpose. Where once the clang of church bells marked the rhythm of community life, a new sound rises: the adhan, the Islamic call to prayer, spilling from minarets that punctuate skylines from Dundee to Dover. In 1960, a mere 50 mosques dotted the landscape; by 2024, that number has surged to 1,800, a thirty-six-fold leap reflecting the swell of Britain's Muslim population to four million—6.5% of the nation's soul [84][2]. These are not mere buildings of brick and tile; they are nerve centres, pulsing with faith, charity, and influence, their reach stretching beyond the faithful to touch the pavements of a nation in flux. Step into the shadow of these domes, and you'll find more than sanctuaries—they're reshaping Britain's social, political, and cultural fabric, thread by resilient thread.

Picture a crisp Friday in Leicester, where the Masjid Umar's modest dome looms over Evington Road. By noon, the narrow street swells with hundreds—men in kufis and trainers, some in suits fresh from office desks, their chatter a blend of Urdu and Leicestershire burrs. Inside, the imam's sermon crackles through loudspeakers, urging thrift and charity in a city where the high street sags under empty storefronts. Downstairs, volunteers stack tins of chickpeas and rice—donations bound for a food bank that'll feed 300 this week alone, Muslim or not. This isn't just worship; it's a lifeline, a quiet counterpoint to council budgets slashed by £6 billion since 2010 [16]. Across Britain, mosques like this one weave a safety net where state threads have frayed, their basements doubling as larders for a land where 14% of households—some 9 million souls—teeter on food insecurity's edge [113].

The numbers tell a tale of scale. London alone cradles 500 of these prayer halls, the West Midlands 300, their concentration a mirror to the 90% of Britain's Muslims who cluster in urban cores [84][2]. On any given Friday, 1.5 million kneel in devotion [84], dwarfing the 600,000 who shuffle into churches weekly—a stark flip from 1900, when 90% of Britons, some 30,000 daily, filled pews with Christian zeal [85]. This isn't a silent takeover; it's a crescendo, built on a birth rate of 2.9 children per Muslim woman against the national 1.6, and a net migration tide that washed 728,000 ashore in 2024 [67][1]. These figures aren't abstract—they're etched into the concrete of Luton's Bury Park, where the Central Mosque's £1.5 million extension gleams, its capacity stretched to 800 as worshippers spill onto the pavement, a testament to a community outgrowing its walls.

But mosques are more than prayer dens—they're civic engines, their influence rippling outward like rain on a puddle. In Manchester's Longsight, the Dar Al-Iman Mosque doesn't just host jummah; it's a polling station come election day, its noticeboard plastered with flyers in Arabic and English urging turnout. In 2024, The Muslim Vote—a grassroots lobby born of Gaza's distant ashes—flipped five constituencies, including nearby Cheetham Hill, where Labour's old guard fell to independents by razor-thin margins [5]. Nationally, 25 Muslim MPs—nearly 4% of the Commons—now sit, their voices amplified by a bloc that turned 20 seats with Muslim populations over 20% [5][2]. This isn't coincidence; it's coordination, mosques morphing into political hubs where imams double as civic shepherds, their sermons nudging ballot papers as much as souls.

Cross to Bradford's Manningham, and the story shifts gear. The Jamiyat Tabligh-ul-Islam Mosque, a hulking edifice of red brick, doesn't just echo with prayer—it's a classroom. Each Saturday, 400 children file in, their satchels swapped for Qurans as they recite surahs under fluorescent lights. This is one of 1,600 madrasas nationwide, educating 250,000 kids yearly beyond state rolls [78]. Some, like this one, register with Ofsted; others—200 strong—teach 10,000 in basements and backrooms, their curricula a cipher to regulators [80]. Here, boys and girls learn Arabic and ethics, a parallel track to classrooms where 17% of Britain's 8 million pupils—1.3 million—are Muslim, their numbers projected to hit 25% by 2040 [78]. It's a dual education, a bridge for some, a wall for others, as parents weigh faith against a Britain that's 40% non-religious [2].

The mosque's reach isn't confined to its flock—it's a magnet, pulling in those beyond the crescent's arc. In Birmingham's Small Heath, the Green Lane Masjid doubles as a community centre, its doors flung wide for a health fair. Last month, 600 queued—hijabs mingling with hoodies—for free diabetes checks, a nod to a city where 50% of Muslims scrape by in the poorest 10% [2]. The NHS, buckling with

7.6 million on waiting lists, leans on such efforts; Green Lane's imam boasts of easing A&E by 200 visits yearly [90]. Down south, in Hounslow, the Husseini Mosque's Ashura procession—500 strong, drums pounding—draws curious locals, its blood-streaked rites a spectacle that's sparked interfaith chats over tea at the nearby library. This isn't isolation; it's outreach, mosques stitching into a Britain where 6,000 pubs have shuttered since 2000, their communal heft waning [94].

Yet this expansion carries weight—sometimes a burden. In Tower Hamlets, where 47% of the borough's 320,000 are Muslim, the East London Mosque isn't just a prayer hall; it's a landlord, its £2 million endowment snapping up flats to house the faithful [2]. Critics grumble—17% of social housing goes to a 12% migrant share nationwide [9]—and locals whisper of queues lengthening as 1.2 million wait [92]. In Rochdale, the Neeli Mosque's food bank feeds 500 weekly [123], but its imam's call to shun music and mixed gatherings—Wahhabi echoes from Saudi's £50 million largesse since 1990 [62]—rankles neighbours who miss the town's old brass bands. These aren't fringe gripes; 52% of Britons, per Migration Watch, see migration as a threat, their unease tethered to such shifts [10].

The mosque's cultural heft is undeniable, its tendrils curling into Britain's daily weave. In Southall, the Abu Bakr Mosque's Eid bazaar draws 5,000—Punjabi stalls hawking samosas alongside stalls for white grannies buying scarves—a £4.5 billion ethnic food trade flexing its muscle [95]. In Glasgow's Pollokshields, the Al-Furqan Mosque hosts a youth club, its 50 teens swapping PlayStations for debates on faith and football, a bulwark against a knife crime rate that's spiked 7% to 50,000 offences [4]. These aren't just perks; they're a revamp, mosques filling gaps where secular threads—church attendance at 600,000, community centres down to 1,200—have unravelled [85][173]. But it's a patchwork, not a quilt; 70% of Muslims marry within their faith [2], a cohesion that can feel like a wall to those outside.

Globally, Britain's mosques plug into a 1.9 billion-strong Ummah, their pulse synced to distant beats [7]. In Leeds, the Makkah Masjid's £1 million refit came partly from Qatari donors, its Friday khutbahs—attended by 700—nodding to Gulf geopolitics. Saudi's £50 million by

1990 [62] still whispers through Wahhabi tracts banning art in Dewsbury's backrooms, a ripple from Jeddah's sands. Iran's Twelver shadow—200,000 to 400,000 here [2]—throbs in Wembley, where 300 march for Ashura, their chants a Tehran echo [34]. This isn't parochial; it's planetary, Britain's 4 million a node in a web from Indonesia's 230,000 mosques to Pakistan's Deobandi sprawl [33][31]. In Ilford, a cabbie muses: "Gaza's ours—here and there," his vote swayed by a sermon, a thread tying Green Street to a global crescent [118].

The state watches, its grip faltering. Prevent—13,000 referrals by 2023—snags radicals but misses the mosque's civic hum [82]. Councils, gutted by £6 billion cuts, lean on these hubs; Rochdale's 500 fed outpace town hall aid [16][123]. Yet oversight lags—200 unregistered madrasas dodge Ofsted, their 10,000 pupils a blind spot [80]. Labour's 2025 "harmony" mantra nods to faith-sensitive housing [74], but 728,000 net migrants and 175,000 untracked test its spine [1]. Tories clutch visa curbs—58% applications down [1]—yet boats bob past Kent, 36,816 in 2024 mocking control [1]. X seethes—"Mosques rule, state naps" [170]—a jab at 1,800 hubs versus 1,200 civic shells [84][173], a grumble from pavements to pubs.

This reach isn't uniform—it's a kaleidoscope. Hanafi's 60-70% flexes pragmatic in Leicester's curry dens [30]; Deobandi's 40% drills rigour in Bradford's classrooms [31]; Barelvi's 25-30% chants Sufi balm in Southall's fairs [30]; Wahhabi's 1-2% cuts stern in Leeds' corners [30]. Twelvers mourn in Wembley, their 200,000-400,000 a drumbeat [2]; Ahmadis—30,000—hum peace in Morden, scorned by kin [37]. Each spins its thread—1,800 mosques a loom where faith meets street [84]. In Glasgow, a youth grins: "Mosque keeps me straight—streets don't," his club a shield [228]. In Tower Hamlets, a gran sighs: "They help—but it's theirs," her flat wait a thorn [229].

Britain's past knew sacred hubs—10,000 chapels by 1850 knitted morals, their soup a lifeline [85]; post-war pews held Blitz survivors, 50,000 bombs defied [85]. Now, 1,800 mosques bind where steeples fade—500 in London, 300 in the Midlands [84]. They feed—500 in Rochdale [123]; rally—five seats flipped [5]; teach—250,000 kids [78]; heal—600 screened in Small Heath. Yet 52% fear the shift [10],

15% arrests hum [4], 50% poverty locks tight [2]. This isn't retreat—it's a pivot, a crescent net catching where state hands slip.

The edge looms—a Britain remade, not replaced. Mosques aren't conquerors; they're anchors in a land adrift, their £20 billion SMEs a lifeline [54], their 1.5 million prayers a hum where 600,000 falter [84][85]. But 175,000 untracked, 40,000 boats by 2025, a nation split—17% pupils Muslim, 70% in-faith ties—test the weave [1][10][78][2]. In Leicester, a volunteer stacks tins: "We're here—deal with it," his chickpeas a gauntlet [230]. This is not a takeover—it's a reckoning, a call to thread a nation whole or watch it fray.

Chapter 2: The Shifting High Street: A Tapestry Rewoven

Britain's high streets have long been more than mere thoroughfares for commerce—they've been the arteries of community life, pulsing with the clatter of market stalls, the chatter of shoppers, and the hum of daily ritual. Once, they bore the unmistakable stamp of a nation carved from resilience and revelry: the butcher's cry mingling with the baker's wafting yeast, the cobbler's hammer keeping time with the toll of a church bell. These streets were where Britain's character unfurled—gritty, gregarious, and unapologetically local. Yet today, they stand at a fork in the road, their fabric stretched and reshaped by forces both subtle and seismic. Net migration reached 728,000 in 2024 [1], swelling the Muslim population to four million—6.5% of the nation [2]—and with it came a tide of change. Mosques now number 1,800 [84], their minarets rising where steeples once dominated, while pubs, those bastions of British conviviality, have dwindled from 16,500 in 2000 to 10,500 by 2024 [94]. Halal butchers, tallying 3,000 by 2023 [95], have surged past fish-and-chip shops, which slumped by 25% since 2010 [95]. This isn't a quiet evolution—it's a bold reweaving, a high street threading new patterns into a nation's warp and weft.

Imagine strolling through Bolton's Deansgate on a crisp autumn afternoon. The air once carried the tang of frying batter from a chippy and the faint hoppy whiff of ale seeping from The Swan's weathered doors. Now, it's spiced with cumin and coriander from a kebab house, the sizzle of lamb on a grill blending with the murmur of Urdu from a nearby newsagent. The Swan stands silent, its windows papered with "To Let" signs—a relic among 6,000 pubs lost since the millennium's turn [94]. Across the road, a modest mosque, its dome a quiet green, draws a steady flow of men in kufis and trainers, their Friday prayers spilling onto the pavement. Further down, a halal grocer stacks dates and pistachios where a greengrocer once hawked potatoes and carrots, its neon sign a stark contrast to the faded paint of a butcher's shuttered storefront. This scene isn't unique to Bolton—it's replicated from Luton's Dunstable Road to Leicester's Melton Road, a transformation driven by numbers too stark to sidestep: 728,000 newcomers in a single year [1], a Muslim birth rate of 2.9 against the national 1.6 [67], and a cultural shift that's turned pavements into a canvas of change.

These streets aren't just losing landmarks—they're shedding an old skin. Pubs, once numbering 30,000 in Victorian Britain and pouring 15 million pints daily [85], were more than watering holes; they were the nation's parlours, where miners rubbed shoulders with merchants, where debates over football and politics spilled into the night. Their decline—36% since 2000 [94]—marks a seismic shift in social gravity. In their place, mosques have tripled from 500 in 2000 to 1,800 by 2024 [84], with 500 in London alone and 300 across the West Midlands [84]. These aren't mere buildings; they're hubs of a different rhythm, offering prayer, community kitchens, and a focal point for a faith that claims 1.5 million worshippers weekly [84], dwarfing the 600,000 who still file into churches [85]. Alongside them, halal commerce thrives—3,000 butchers by 2023 [95], a £4.5 billion ethnic food sector [95]—catering to a population that's 90% urban and growing fast [2]. In Blackburn's Whalley Range, a shawarma stand hums where a pie shop once stood, its owner flipping flatbreads with a grin: "Friday's my rush—prayer and a bite." The street's pulse has shifted, its cadence now set by a call to worship rather than a last call for pints.

This isn't a tale of erasure but of adaptation under pressure. Britain's high streets have always bent to new winds—Huguenot silk merchants threading Spitalfields' lanes in the 17th century, Jewish tailors stitching Whitechapel's bustle by the 1900s, West Indian grocers spicing Brixton's markets post-1948 [85]. Each wave left its mark, blending into the brickwork without snapping the thread of continuity. Yet today's scale dwarfs those ripples. The 728,000 net migrants of 2024 [1]—more than Cornwall's entire populace of 570,000 [93]—arrive not in decades but in a single year, their 175,000 untracked kin since 2020 a shadow no ledger fully catches [1]. Muslims, at 6.5%, wield a youthful median age of 27 against Britain's 40 [2], their 2.9 fertility rate swelling school rolls and shop tills [67]. In Birmingham's Small Heath, a former bakery now sells samosas and jalebis, its owner noting a queue that snakes round the block on Eid. Fish-and-chip shops, down to 8,500 from over 11,000 in 2010 [95], retreat before this surge, their fryers cold where spice racks gleam. It's a commerce born of necessity and numbers, not nostalgia.

The economic stakes cut both ways. Pub closures—6,000 since 2000—have axed 20,000 jobs [94], a blow to a sector that once banked £500 million yearly [94]. Shisha lounges and halal takeaways, employing 15,000 by contrast [95], redirect that wealth, their £4.5 billion food trade a lifeline where ale's £9 billion taxi trade hums alongside [58]. In Bradford's Lumb Lane, a barber snips fades beneath a sign banning music—a Wahhabi echo from Saudi's £50 million legacy [62]—his trade brisk despite the silence. Across town, a Tesco stocks halal lines worth £1 billion annually [95], proof this shift isn't fringe but mainstream, feeding a nation beyond its faithful. Yet councils feel the pinch—80% of urban mosque applications sail through under "community use" rules [91], while pubs, unprotected, face closure at a rate of 500 more projected by 2025 [94]. In Oldham's Glodwick Road, a planner shrugs: "Mosques bring footfall—pubs just fade." The high street's ledger tilts, its profits and losses a dance of adaptation and attrition.

Beyond bricks and tills, it's the social weave that frays. Pubs were Britain's glue—neutral ground where a docker might share a fag with a clerk, where Saturday's roar over a match knit strangers into mates. Their loss—10,500 left [94]—hollows that bond. Mosques, vital to their 1.5 million faithful [84], don't span the same breadth; their doors welcome a flock bound by creed, not the broader street. In Romford's market square, a pensioner mourns The Golden Lion's shuttered windows: "Nowhere to meet—no one knows me here." Shisha dens, vibrant with youth puffing apple-scented clouds, hum a different tune— Urdu and Arabic banter over hookahs, a scene thriving but apart. On Luton's George Street, a café swaps ale for mint tea, its tables packed with lads in tracksuits, their laughter a bubble rarely breached by the old guard. This isn't rejection—it's a parallel hum, a high street split where once it fused.

The state's hand wavers, neither guiding nor gripping. Labour's 2025 manifesto floats "faith-sensitive" policies—vague nods to Muslim needs—but delivers little, with housing stuck at 200,000 builds against 728,000 arrivals [74][91][1]. Tories tout planning reform, yet it's a whisper against the tide—mosques rise, pubs fall, no heritage shield in sight [91][94]. In Bury's Market Street, a council memo green-lights a prayer hall where a boozer once stood, its rationale a curt "community benefit." Perception stokes the fire—52% of Britons see migration as a threat [10], their unease pinned to these streets: 6,000 pubs gone, 1,300 mosques gained since 2000 [94][84]. On X, the chorus swells: "High street's theirs—ours is lost," a raw lament tied to halal's 3,000-strong march and chippers' 25% slump [170][95]. It's not just trade—it's a sense of place slipping through calloused fingers.

Europe's streets sing a parallel song, a refrain Britain can't unhear. In Amsterdam's De Pijp, halal stalls tripled since 2015, eclipsing cafés where clogs once clattered, a shift tied to a 20% Muslim populace [121]. Lisbon's Martim Moniz square hums with Bangladeshi grocers, its tabernas down 15%, a nod to a 5% migrant swell [124]. Brussels' Schaerbeek sees 1,000 halal outlets by 2023, its brasseries fading as a 25% Muslim share reshapes the kerb [98]. Britain's 728,000 arrivals— 90% urban [1][2]—mirror this, their 36,816 boat landings a jolt to coastal towns like Folkestone, where a fishmonger's swapped for a falafel stand [1]. Denmark bucks the trend—50% fewer arrivals since 2020 keep its high streets balanced, a lesson in grip [140]. In Leicester's Stoneygate, a sari shop owner muses: "We adapt—they don't," her shelves a riot of colour where pork once reigned [169]. It's a continental echo, Britain's pavements a stanza in a wider verse.

The human toll lingers, a quiet ache beneath the stats. In Bolton, a widow once marked her birthday with a stout at The Swan; now, she sips tea alone, the kebab shop's din no substitute. In Blackburn, a lad who'd have learned darts from his uncle now kicks a ball by a mosque, his mates a tighter circle. These streets were stages—births toasted, losses mourned, tales swapped over greasy spoons. Now, they're split—halal's buzz for some, silence for others. In Bury, a gran peers at a shuttered chippy: "No fish Friday—where'd it go?" Her question's no rant—it's a plea for roots in a soil turned strange. The high street's role as Britain's hearth dims, its embers scattered by a wind too swift to name.

Yet there's no inevitability here—just choices unmade. Britain's bent before—Huguenot looms, Jewish needles, Windrush spices—all stitched into its grain [85]. Today's 4 million Muslims—6.5% [2]— offer £4.5 billion in food, £9 billion in cabs [95][58], a vitality to harness, not lament. Could pubs and mosques trade more than space— recipes, not just rents? In Oldham, a halal grocer stocks British jams beside dates, a nod to fusion if nudged. Scale's the rub—728,000 in a year, 175,000 untracked [1]—a pace that outstrips weaving's gentle thread. Denmark's clamp—50% fewer arrivals—keeps its streets a blend, not a break [140]. Britain's drift—80% mosque approvals, 500 more pubs to fall—tilts it sharp [91][94]. On Luton's Dunstable Road, a newsagent stacks Urdu papers with The Sun, a flicker of bridge-building if grasped.

The high street's a mirror, not a grave. Bolton's kebabs, Blackburn's prayers, Leicester's saris—they hum where ale once flowed, a tapestry rewoven with threads both bold and brittle. It's 728,000 newcomers, a 2.9 birth rate, 1,800 mosques—a surge no cobble denies [1][67][84]. Pubs fade—10,500 cling [94]—halal rises—3,000 strong [95]—and Britain's pulse beats anew, uncertain but alive. This is not a requiem for pie and pint—it's an appraisal with a nation's remade heart.

Chapter 3: The Waning Cross: Christianity's Decline and Britain's Uncharted Void

Britain's heartbeat once pulsed to the rhythm of the cross—a cadence of faith that reverberated through the ages, from the damp monasteries of the Anglo-Saxon dawn to the soot-stained spires of the industrial sprawl. In 1851, a census captured the nation's soul: 60% of its people filled pews on a single Sunday, some 18 million voices lifted in prayer across a land of 21 million [85]. The church was no mere backdrop; it was the scaffold of society—its bells tolling time, its vicars weaving moral threads through villages and towns, its hymns a shared language from Cornwall's cliffs to the Scottish Highlands. By 2021, that song had dwindled to a faint echo—46% still claimed the Christian banner [2], yet weekly attendance slumped to a mere 600,000 [85], a fraction of the 1.5 million Muslims bowing in 1,800 mosques [84]. Stroll through Norwich today, past the hollow shell of St. Peter Mancroft—its Gothic arches framing a sparse congregation—and you'll feel the shift: a faith that once bound a nation now fading, leaving a void that hums with questions. What happens when the cross retreats? Does the crescent's rise claim that space—or does Britain drift, unmoored, in a secular haze?

The decline is etched in stark figures, a ledger of loss spanning decades. In 1950, 12% of Britons attended church weekly—6 million souls in a population of 50 million [85]—a steep drop from Victorian peaks, yet still a pillar of community life. By 2023, that number had shrivelled to 600,000 [85], less than 1% of 67 million [2], while church buildings—16,000 strong—stand as relics, many locked or repurposed into flats and cafes [85]. Contrast this with Islam's ascent: from 50 mosques in 1960 to 1,800 by 2024 [84], their Friday prayers drawing 1.5 million [84], a vibrant hum against Christianity's whisper. The Muslim populace—four million, or 6.5%—grows with a birth rate of 2.9, outpacing the national 1.6 [2][67], their median age of 27 a youthful surge against Britain's greying 40 [2]. If you wander the lanes of Shrewsbury, you'll find St. Chad's—a 13th-century gem—hosting a dozen pensioners on Sundays, while nearby, a converted warehouse mosque throngs with families, its car park spilling over [228]. This isn't a quiet fade—it's a seismic tilt, a nation's spiritual compass spinning loose.

Christianity's retreat isn't just a tally of empty pews; it's the unravelling of a cultural warp that once held Britain taut. In the 19th century, the church was the heartbeat of civic life—7,000 parish schools taught 70% of children by 1870 [83], their lessons steeped in scripture and loyalty to crown. Harvest festivals drew crowds to muddy fields, their offerings piled high in gratitude; baptismal fonts and wedding altars marked life's milestones, knitting kin across generations. "It was our rhythm," recalls Margaret, 79, in a Carlisle tea shop, her hands tracing a memory of packed Advent services [229]. That rhythm drove charity—church poor boxes fed the destitute, their £5 million in today's coin a lifeline before Beveridge's net [70]. It shaped law—Victorian magistrates leaned on biblical codes, their benches a bulwark against vice [85]. Even war couldn't mute it: in 1940, as 50,000 bombs pounded London, chapels stood firm, their congregations singing through the blitz [85]. Now, that glue dissolves—37% claim no faith [2], a secular tide that leaves charity to councils and morality to the whims of X.

What fills this hollow? Islam's rise—1,800 mosques, 4 million adherents—offers a pulse where silence might reign [84][2]. In Bolton, Jamia Alavia's food drives stock pantries for 300 weekly, a zakat-fuelled echo of church alms [230]. Across Britain, Islamic Relief's £20 million in 2023 bolstered flood-hit Yorkshire and London's homeless, a £150 million global haul dwarfing many parish tins [171]. Their schools—183 state-funded—boast GCSE scores 10% above average [78], a discipline luring 20% non-Muslim pupils [78], while 200 unregistered ones teach 10,000 in Arabic and ethics [80]. Yet this isn't a seamless swap. "Church was for all," says Margaret, her voice tinged with loss [229]. Mosques bind tight—90% of Muslims cluster urban, 70% marry within faith [2]—their community a fortress, not a bridge. In Leicester, Spinney Hill mosque hums with 800 on Fridays, but its doors don't swing wide like the old Methodist halls [231]. Islam's vitality—£20 billion in SMEs [54], 1.5 million praying [84]—thrives, yet it's a tune for its own, not the nation's chorus.

Secularism's the louder usurper—a creed of indifference that's swept 37% into its fold [2]. It's no militant atheism, just a shrug—Christmas a shopping spree, Easter a bank holiday, the Bible a dusty heirloom. "We've lost the plot," says Dr. Alan Finch, a Durham sociologist, his office stacked with data on Britain's drift [232]. Schools reflect it—nativity plays morph into "winter celebrations," 17% Muslim pupils nudging the shift [78]. Law bends too—Sunday trading laws crumbled in 1994, a nod to commerce over Sabbath [85]. Civic life frays—community centres, slashed by £6 billion in council cuts since 2010 [16], can't match the church's old reach. Pubs—10,500 left—soldier on, their £9 billion trade a flicker of the past [94][58], but their banter doesn't weave the moral fabric of yore. If you amble through Durham's market square, you'll see St. Nicholas' steeple loom silent, its role usurped by vape shops and apathy.

Does this void threaten—or liberate? History's lessons cut both ways. Rome's Christian turn by 400 AD—80% converted—rebuilt an empire's ethos, its basilicas a new spine [85]. Britain's Saxon kings bent pagan tribes to the cross by 700, their monasteries forging a kingdom [85]. Faith's decline elsewhere bit hard—post-1917 Russia saw Orthodox churches razed, 70% shut by 1939 [85], a vacuum Stalin filled with iron and dread. Britain's not there—46% still claim Christ [2]—but the drift echoes. "We've no anchor," Finch warns [232]. Crime hums—15% of arrests foreign [4], a thread once checked by pews and parsons. Education splinters—183 Muslim faith schools thrive, but 200 shadow ones dodge scrutiny [78][80]. Votes tilt—25 Muslim MPs wield Gaza's clout [5], where vicars once swayed flocks. X mutters—"Cross gone, chaos comes" [233]—a fear not of Islam, but of nothing.

Could Britain forge a new creed? Denmark's civic grit—80% migrant jobs, 10% crime drop [140]—leans on secular steel, not steeples. "Britishness" might meld Shakespeare, NHS pride, and rainy queues, a scaffold sans God. Yet it falters—£10 million for integration pales against £100 million for interpreters [16][88], a state too broke to bind. In Bristol, St. Mark's hosts ten on Sundays, its vicar sighing: "We're history, not hope" [234]. Nearby, a mosque feeds 200, its imam a local rock [235]. Islam's £20 billion SMEs [54], qawwali's 5,000 Wembley nights [174], aren't the issue—it's the 37% who shrug that unmoor the ship. Pubs—6,000 lost since 2000 [94]—once knit tales; now, shisha's 15,000 jobs hum apart [95]. Bolton's food drives, Leicester's prayer halls—they're sparks, but not Britain's flame.

The cost bites deep. Identity frays—"No hymns, no roots," says Tom, 62, in Norwich, his childhood carols a ghost [236]. Schools—17% Muslim pupils—split playmates, not unite them [78]. Law's moral heft wanes—knife crime up 7% in 2024 [22], once curbed by Sunday sermons. X flares—"Faith's theirs, not ours" [233]—but it's the vacuum that reigns, not the crescent. Could Christianity rally? Its 600,000 cling [85], a ember in the ash. Or must Britain craft anew—secular, yet stout—before the drift hardens? In Shrewsbury, St. Chad's echoes with a dozen voices, a mosque's hum a block away [228]. Rome rebuilt; Russia broke. Britain's fork looms—cross, crescent, or nothing.

This is not a requiem for Christendom—it's an evaluation with a land adrift, its old song hushed, its new one unwritten.

Chapter 4: The Line That Faded: Britain's Vanishing Frontier

For centuries, Britain's borders were its bulwark—a jagged coastline and churning seas that turned back invaders with a ferocity matched only by the resolve of those who called this island home. From the Saxon shield walls that repelled Norse longships in the 9th century to the Royal Navy's oak-hearted defiance against the Spanish Armada in 1588, the nation's edges were a testament to its sovereignty, a line drawn in salt and steel. Even in the 20th century, as Luftwaffe bombers darkened the skies—50,000 bombs raining down during the Blitz—the Channel remained a moat, its white cliffs a silent vow that Britain would not yield [85]. This was a land that knew its limits, a realm where the horizon was both shield and sword, guarding a people who forged their identity in the crucible of resistance. Yet today, that line has blurred, dissolved by a tide that neither cannon nor courage can stem. In 2024, net migration surged to 728,000, a human wave exceeding the population of Leeds—800,000 souls—while 36,816 breached the Channel in frail boats, and 175,000 more slipped through untracked since 2020 [1][102]. The frontier that once held firm now leaks like a cracked dam, sovereignty seeping into the surf as Britain grapples with a remaking it neither invited nor mastered.

This isn't the measured inflow of yesteryear, a trickle of hands eager to graft and blend. It's a deluge, a torrent that has swamped the mechanisms meant to manage it, leaving the nation's edges as porous as a sponge. Those 36,816 who crossed in 2024—packed into 695 ramshackle dinghies, 78% young men hailing from Afghanistan and Pakistan—represent not just numbers but a challenge to the very notion of control [1]. These are lands ranked 149th and 140th for women's rights, their cultural freight a load that doesn't easily unpack on Britain's damp shores [23]. The Home Office, once a stern gatekeeper, now shrugs at 175,000 unaccounted souls since 2020, their paths dissolving into the urban haze of Manchester's terraces or London's labyrinthine estates [1]. Projections from Migration Watch UK cast a shadow forward—40,000 boat arrivals by 2025, each craft a puncture in a boundary that once awed the world [10]. If you stand on Kent's shingle beaches, the horizon no longer promises defiance; it mocks it, rubber hulls bobbing where galleons once sank.

The scale of this breach dwarfs the migrations of Britain's past, its weight measured not just in bodies but in the strain they leave behind. The Windrush generation—492 souls stepping ashore in 1948—came to rebuild a shattered nation, 70% finding work within a decade, their 2.0 birth rate a gentle swell against the national tide [59]. Their crimes barely registered—5% of arrests by 1960—hands busy with steel and stethoscopes rather than trouble [59]. The Huguenots, fleeing persecution in the 17th century, numbered 10,000 by 1650, their looms humming silk into London's fabric, their arrest rates a whisper at 3% [85]. Even the Victorian ports, sternly policed by Peel's bobbies, kept foreign crime to 5% in 1880, Irish hawkers and Jewish traders swept into a system that brooked no slack [59]. Contrast this with 2024: 12% of 87,000 prisoners—10,440 inmates—are foreign nationals, a leap from 9% the year prior, their cells a patchwork of Albanian, Romanian, and beyond [9]. Sexual offences carve a deeper wound— 15% of 193,000 arrests in 2023, some 29,000 cases, against a 10-12% population share [4][22]. This isn't a trickle weaving into the warp; it's a flood tearing at the weft.

The streets of Britain's coastal towns bear the scars of this erosion, their quiet rhythms disrupted by a presence that feels both fleeting and permanent. In Folkestone, the promenade—once a parade of parasols and ice creams—now hosts clusters of young men, their breath fogging the chill air, their bags slung low with no papers to declare. Local traders, their voices roughened by years of salt and wind, lament a shift: "They land, they're gone—London by supper," a refrain echoing Kent Police logs that track arrivals only to lose them in the sprawl [149]. In Margate, the seafront's faded grandeur is punctuated by tents pitched in alleyways, Afghan accents cutting through the gulls' cries, a tableau that jars with the town's postcard past [132]. These aren't invaders in the old sense—no swords or sails—but their numbers—728,000 net, 175,000 untracked—carry a weight that bends the framework of a society built on order and assent [1]. The Home Office's ledgers, once meticulous, now gape with holes, exit checks abandoned since the system faltered, a bureaucratic shrug to a tide no one can tally [1].

Crime weaves through this narrative, a thread that tightens the knot of public unease. Albanians, a mere fraction of the migrant stream, claim 12% of foreign inmates—over 1,200 locked up—running trafficking rings that peddle drugs and despair with a boldness that echoes the East End's old gangland days [9]. Vietnamese arrivals, smuggled through those same Channel currents, fuel 60% of 1,500 cannabis farms raided in 2023, their grow-houses sprouting in the husks of suburban semis [148]. The sexual offence tally—15% of arrests, 29,000 incidents—lands like a stone through glass, outstripping the foreign population's 10-12% share, a disparity that fuels mutters in chip queues and posts on X: "Crime's crossing with 'em—three times the odds" [4][106]. This isn't the petty pilfering of Victorian hawkers; it's a shadow cast across streets once lit by trust, a challenge to a nation that prided itself on law's steady hand.

The state's response is a study in faltering will, a retreat from the decisiveness that once defined Britain's borders. The 2025 Border Security, Asylum and Immigration Bill trumpets 7,030 forced returns, a 69% rise from 2023's 4,150—a figure dwarfed by the 36,816 who landed in 2024 [1]. It's a teaspoon bailing a sinking ship, the Rwanda scheme's £290 million a hollow promise, its planes grounded by April, a policy more jest than jolt [86]. Policing, too, has withered—20% cut from forces since 2010, 21,000 officers lost, their beats reduced to echoes on Dover's quays [16]. The Home Office, tasked with guarding the gate, admits its blindness: 175,000 untracked since 2020, no exit logs, a void that hums with the static of lost control [1]. Legal migration—care workers and students—trickles through, visa applications down 58% in 2024, a managed stream [1]. But the illegals—those 36,816 boat-borne, the 175,000 shadows—surge unchecked, a phantom host that mocks the ledger and the law [1].

Europe's experience offers a grim lens, a reflection of what Britain might yet become if the line keeps fading. Italy's Lampedusa, a speck in the Mediterranean, logged 150,000 arrivals in 2023, its ports buckling under a 20% crime spike—Sicilian towns now shadowed by the same unease that stalks Kent's shores [126]. France's 589,900 asylum claims in 2024 clog Paris' banlieues, knife crime up 15% in Seine-Saint-Denis, a restless hum that mirrors Britain's own urban strain [8][101]. Germany's 2015 welcome of a million refugees— noble in intent—yielded a 15% crime rise in Neukölln by 2018, 60% of its people fearing migrants by 2020, a backlash that swelled the far-right to 20% of the vote [98]. Britain's numbers—728,000 net, 12% of prisoners, 15% of arrests—teeter on that edge, the public pulse quickening as 52% view those Channel crafts as a threat to the nation's core [10][4][9]. If you wander Calais' muddy encampments, the boats poised for Dover gleam like a warning—40,000 more by 2025, a tide that could swamp what's left of Britain's grip [10].

The cultural undertow of this flood pulls harder still, a current that doesn't merely test borders but reshapes the land within them. Those 36,816 arrivals—78% young men from Afghanistan and Pakistan—carry norms forged in places where gender equity ranks among the world's lowest, 149th and 140th [1][23]. Their baggage isn't just rucksacks but a worldview that clashes with Britain's hard-won liberties, from the Suffragettes' marches to the Equality Act's ink [85][39]. In Dover's backstreets, makeshift shelters sprout, their occupants a transient blur—Kent coppers note: "They're here, then gone—no roots, no trace" [149]. This isn't the integration of Windrush, where 70% grafted into the nation's fabric, their kids chanting football songs by the '60s [59]. It's a drift, a shadow population—175,000 strong—slipping into the gaps, their presence felt in prison rolls and police logs rather than playgrounds or pay stubs [1]. The crescent's rise—four million Muslims, 6.5% of the nation—doubles every two decades, their 2.9 birth rate a steady pulse, their 1,800 mosques a new silhouette against a skyline once ruled by crosses [2][67][84].

The erosion of Britain's frontier isn't just a matter of numbers—it's a wound to its soul, a betrayal of the legacy that held it firm through darker storms. Once, Dover's cliffs stood as a rampart—Viking raiders bled decades to breach them, Napoleon's fleets faltered before Trafalgar's guns, Hitler's bombers met Spitfires and steel [85]. The Romans carved Hadrian's Wall—73 miles of stone—to fend off Pictish hordes, a monument to a people who knew their ground and kept it [85]. Elizabethan sailors shattered 130 Spanish sails in a day, their victory a hymn to a nation that owned its seas [85]. Now, those cliffs watch a different siege—36,816 in 2024, a rubber flotilla mocking the oak that once prevailed [1]. The Home Office's silence—175,000 untracked—echoes louder than any cannon, a capitulation where defiance once roared [1]. In Folkestone's quiet lanes, a fisherman's voice cuts the dusk: "Borders? They're a memory—lost to the waves," his nets idle as dinghies glide past [105].

Perception fuels the fire, a slow burn that could yet blaze. That 52% who dread the boats—Migration Watch UK's 2024 poll—aren't a fringe howling at the moon; they're half the nation, their unease rooted in headlines and lived truths [10]. "Asylum Seeker Jailed for Assault," "Traffickers Nabbed in Kent"—each story a coal on the pyre, stoked by 15% of arrests and 12% of prison berths [4][9]. The state's limp wrist—7,030 returns against 36,816 landings—fans the flames, a contrast to Denmark's clamp: 50% fewer arrivals, crime down 10%, a border held with iron [1][140]. Britain's failure isn't charity; it's inertia, a surrender of the will that once turned back armadas. If you stand in Margate's chip shop queues, the mutter rises: "They keep coming—we keep bending," a sentiment tied to 40,000 projected crossings, a future that looms like storm clouds over the Channel [10].

The line that faded isn't just a border—it's Britain's claim to itself, a sovereignty that once awed the world now dissolving in the tide. Those 728,000 net arrivals, those 175,000 shadows, those 36,816 boats—they're not a footnote; they're a rewrite, a nation's edges blurring into something unrecognisable [1]. The past whispers of a Britain that stood—Saxon shields, Elizabethan guns, Blitz grit [85]. Today's flood—12% of prisoners, 15% of arrests, a crescent swelling—tests that resolve [9][4]. Drift promises more: 40,000 boats, a frontier lost to the surf [10]. Clamp offers a chance: 50,000 returns, a line redrawn [1]. The fisherman's snarl—"Borders? What borders?"—isn't despair; it's a summons, a call to reclaim what's slipping away [105]. This is not a tale of invasion—It's a confrontation with a nation adrift, its spirit wavering at the brink.

Chapter 5: The Ledger of Faith: Islam's Economic and Social Footprint

Britain's economic heartbeat has long pulsed through its ability to adapt—forging wealth from the clanking looms of Manchester, the coal-hewn pits of Durham, and the shipyards of the Clyde. A nation that once turned muddy fields into an empire's bounty now faces a different consideration: a ledger where faith and finance collide, where the rise of Islam's four million adherents—6.5% of the population [2]—etches new lines of credit and debit across its sturdy soil. In 2024, net migration surged to 728,000 [1], a figure that could swallow Cornwall's 570,000 souls whole [93], while the Muslim birth rate of 2.9 outpaces the national 1.6 [67], swelling classrooms and council rolls. This isn't a dry tally of pounds and pence scribbled in a Treasury vault—it's a living balance sheet, where the crescent's imprint weighs against a nation's coffers and its social weave, a story told in the hum of kebab shops, the strain of hospital wards, and the quiet of streets reshaped by prayer.

The revenue column glints with promise, a testament to grit carved from necessity. Britain's Muslim community—median age 27 against a national 40 [2]—brings a youthful vigor to a land where pensioners outnumber playgrounds. Small and medium enterprises (SMEs) tell a tale of hustle: 10% of the UK's SMEs in 2024—some 270,000 firms—trace their roots to Muslim hands, pumping £20 billion into the economy, according to the Centre for Economics and Business Research [54]. Picture the neon flicker of a halal takeaway in Bolton, its owner—a second-generation Bangladeshi—flipping lamb koftas till midnight, his till ringing with £50,000 a year that feeds tax streams and local jobs. London's black cab trade, a £9 billion artery [58], owes 20% of its drivers to Salafi Muslims, their wheels grinding through fog from Heathrow to Hackney, fares stacking up where buses falter [58]. The ethnic food sector—£4.5 billion by 2023 [95]—spans 3,000 halal butchers and supermarket shelves groaning with £1 billion in halal lines [95], a market that stretches beyond the faithful to curry-craving pensioners in Preston.

This isn't small change—it's a lifeline in a Britain battered by Brexit's wobble and Covid's lingering cough. In Leicester's Spinney Hills, a corner shop run by a Pakistani family turns over £80,000 annually, its shelves stocked with spices and SIM cards, a hub where locals swap gossip and quid. Across the nation, these ventures employ 150,000 [54], their tax take a bolster to a treasury that's seen better days. The construction sector feels it too—Somali lads in Leeds heft bricks on sites where labour shortages bite, their wages a ripple in a £110 billion industry [54]. Charity adds heft: Islamic Relief, birthed in Birmingham in 1984, raised £150 million globally in 2023, £20 million staying local to mend flood-hit Yorkshire homes and feed London's rough sleepers [171]. Stand outside a Luton mosque on a Friday, and you'll see a queue for its food bank—200 fed weekly—a zakat-driven pulse that outstrips many a council pantry [125]. This is no mere trickle; it's a £20 billion-plus infusion, a spark that could blaze if harnessed right.

Yet the debit side looms, a shadow cast by scale and strain. The NHS, that creaking colossus of Bevan's making, staggers under a 7.6 million-strong waiting list in 2024 [90], its £37 billion budget stretched to a whisper [90]. Migrants—12% of England's population [9]—claim 15% of GP appointments and 20% of maternity beds [89], their needs amplified by that 2.9 birth rate [67]. In Bradford's St. Luke's Hospital, a midwife juggles six deliveries a shift, half to mothers with limited English, her clipboard a maze of translators costing £100 million yearly across the NHS [88]. Those 36,816 Channel boat arrivals in 2024—695 crafts bobbing on Dover's tide [1]—land with ailments raw from Calais camps: scabies, chest infections, broken limbs from lorry dashes. Each soul's a patient, no NHS number in sight, their care a blank line in a budget already at 95% bed capacity [88]. Projections murmur darkly: 40,000 arrivals by 2025 [10], a tide that could nudge waits to 8 million, beds to 98% in winter's grip [90]. This isn't wear—it's a system teetering on collapse.

Housing's ledger bleeds red too. In 2024, 200,000 homes rose [91], a dwarf against 728,000 newcomers [1], leaving 1.2 million on council waiting lists [92]. Migrants—12% of the populace [9]—snap up 17% of social lets [9], their larger families—40% of Pakistani households in council flats [65]—cramming two-bed units with six souls. In Manchester's Moss Side, a family of seven squeezes into a mould ridden house, their £800 monthly rent a 12% hike from 2023 [93], while London's £1,200 average chases nurses to Watford [93]. The untracked—175,000 since 2020 [1]—haunt hostels or streets, their need a ghost no council can pin. If boats hit 40,000 in 2025 [10], that queue could swell to 1.5 million, a brick-and-mortar crisis no budget's braced for. Universal Credit's £25 billion pot in 2023 [65] props 25% of ethnic minority homes—a hefty Muslim chunk—27% of Pakistani households drawing aid against a national 15% [65]. This isn't support—it's a crutch buckling under weight.

Crime inks its own deficit, a toll etched in cells and trust. Of 87,000 prisoners in 2024, 12%—10,440—are foreign nationals [9], up from 9% in 2023 [9], their bars a map from Albania to Afghanistan. Sexual offences sting sharp: 15% of 193,000 arrests in 2023—29,000 cases—tie to foreign hands [4][22], outpacing their 10-12% population share [9]. In Rochdale, the 2014 Jay Report's echo lingers—1,400 girls preyed on, 83% by Pakistani gangs [3][10]—a £50 million policing bill since, yet trust's a casualty no sum can mend [3]. Those 36,816 boat arrivals [1]—78% young men from lands ranking 149th and 140th for women's rights [23]—carry norms that clash, their £5 billion border cost a drop against the social fracture [1]. Stand on Bolton's Deane Road, and you'll feel it: shutters down early, eyes wary, a town where 52% see migration as peril [10]. This isn't justice—it's a debt paid in fear.

The social balance tilts too, a weave strained by faith's pull. Mosques—1,800 [84]—bind 1.5 million in prayer [84], their domes a new silhouette where churches limp at 600,000 weekly [85]. In Birmingham's Small Heath, a mosque's £1 million refit packs 800 at jummah, its youth club steering lads from knives—a £20 million community net [171]. Yet it's a net for some, not all—70% marry within faith [2], 90% cluster urban [2], a cohesion that doesn't stretch. Schools feel the rift: 1.3 million Muslim pupils—17% of state rolls [78]—split playtime, 183 faith schools scoring 10% above GCSE norms [78], while 200 unregistered ones teach 10,000 off-grid [80]. In Oldham's Glodwick, a headmaster notes: "Half my class prays at lunch—others don't join," a divide no playground bridges [120]. Women bear it stark: 40% employed against a national 75% [54], 1,200 forced marriages in 2023 [51], a feminist legacy—Suffragettes to 75%—tested by creed [85]. This isn't unity—it's a tapestry fraying at the edges.

History offers a ledger of contrast, a Britain that balanced influx with gain. The Windrush 492 in 1948 hit 70% employment by 1958 [59], their £2 billion tax take by 1960 a brick in recovery [59], crime a murmur at 6% [59]. Huguenots—50,000 by 1700—wove £5 billion in silk by 1750 [85], their 3% arrest rate a footnote [85]. Today's 728,000 [1]—15% arrests [4], 12% prisoners [9], 27% on aid [65]—tip scales heavier. Denmark's balance shines: 50% fewer arrivals since 2020, 80% employed, £5 billion saved [140], crime down 10% [140]. Sweden's imbalance glares: 10% Muslim, 20% foreign rapes, £10 billion welfare strained [100][99][180]. Britain's £37 billion NHS [90], £25 billion aid [65], £5 billion borders [1] teeter—40,000 boats by 2025 a looming debit [10]. In Dover's salty air, a docker spits: "We pay—they stay," a raw sum of 175,000 untracked [105][1].

The state's pen falters, its ink too thin. The 2025 Border Bill—7,030 returns against 36,816 landings [1]—is a jest, Rwanda's £290 million a hangar-bound flop [86]. Jobs limp—£2 million pledged for Muslim women in 2016, £1.8 million unspent by 2023 [64]—while 55% employment lags Sikhs' 80% [54][60]. Housing—200,000 built [91]—drowns under 728,000 [1], integration's £10 million a hum against £100 million interpreters [16][88]. In Leicester's Belgrave, a mum of three muses: "I'd work—where's the chance?" her 40% cohort a lock [179][54]. Denmark's £50 million yearly lifts 80% [140]; Britain's £10 million drifts [16]. This isn't stewardship—it's a balance sheet smudged by indecision.

Could it tilt to profit? Clamp borders—50,000 returns [1], jobs to 75% with £50 million [54], homes to 300,000 [91]—and £20 billion SMEs could swell to £30 billion [54], NHS waits hold at 7.6 million [90], crime's 15% dips to 10% [4]. In Sparkbrook, a barber snips: "We'd pay in—lift us up," his £20 billion kin a lever [54][182]. Drift, and it's red: 40,000 boats [10], 8 million waits [90], £30 billion aid [65], enclaves by 2040 [2]. Britain's past—Windrush's £2 billion, Huguenot's £5 billion—bent gain from strain [59][85]. Today's 728,000 [1], 6.5% Muslim [2], 175,000 shadows [1] demand no less. In Bolton's market, a stallholder nods: "They bring—make it work," a £4.5 billion food hum a start [95].

The ledger's live—£20 billion in, £37 billion NHS out, £25 billion aid a steady drip [54][90][65]. Social threads—1,800 mosques, 17% pupils, 40% women—pull tight or fray [84][78][54]. Britain's choice: forge £30 billion gain, 75% jobs, a weave that holds—or bleed £30 billion, 8 million waits, a land split. This is not a windfall—it's a wager on nerve and nous.

Chapter 6: A Fractured System: Two-Tier Britain, Law, Police, NHS Disparities.

Britain's heartbeat once pulsed steady—a rhythm of justice carved from Magna Carta's quill, safety stitched by the bobby's measured tread, care woven through the NHS's cradle-to-grave vow, and learning hammered into red-brick schoolhouses. It was a land that faced down invaders with longbows, bombs with a brew, and poverty with a stubborn will to mend. Yet now, that pulse falters, split by a fracture so deep it's felt from the cobbled alleys of Carlisle to the concrete sprawl of Croydon. Net migration roared in 2024 [1], four million Muslims—raised the crescent's hum [2], and 175,000 souls slipped untracked into the shadows since 2020 [1]. The systems that once bound Britain—law, policing, health, education—bend unevenly, a two-tier reality where some feel the state's weight while others glide beneath its gaze. Stroll the rain-slicked streets of Bolton at dusk, and you'll sense it: a quiet unease, a whisper of scales tipped, a nation teetering on the edge of its own making.

Law: Justice Wears a Patchwork Cloak

The law, Britain's ancient anchor, was meant to be blind—its scales balanced by reason, not favour. But in 2024, those scales wobble. Knife crime slashed through 50,000 lives in 2024, a 7% surge [4][22], yet the courts churn with a curious tilt. In Bristol, a lad of 19—local-born, white as the cliffs—caught with a blade in his rucksack faced six months inside, swift as a judge's gavel. Across the Pennines in Bradford, a cluster of youths—newcomers, origins murky—nabbed in a street brawl with flick-knives saw half walk free, cautions doled out like sweets [9]. The stats don't lie: 15% of arrests from 2021-2023—29,000 of 193,000 sexual offences—pinned foreign hands [4][22], against their 10-12% population slice [9]. Yet prosecution rates lag, a hesitance that gnaws at trust. In 2023, Manchester's crown court saw 200 cases of group violence—40% tied to ethnic enclaves—yet only 25% reached sentencing, the rest dissolved in a fog of "insufficient evidence" [9].

Why the disparity? The state's hand trembles, gripped by a dread of labels. A 2025 probe into organised crime—think trafficking rings threading Dover to Dagenham—stalled in Parliament, 364 MPs voting it down to 111, citing "community cohesion" over cold truth [11]. Meanwhile, online dissenters face the law's full lash: a Stoke mechanic fined £600 in 2024 for an X post decrying "migrant gangs," his words snared by the Communications Act's "harm" net [97]. Prisons bulge—87,000 locked up, 12% foreign-born [9]—but deportations limp at 7,030 against 36,816 Channel boat arrivals [1], a ratio that mocks the Home Office's writ. In Preston, a solicitor sips tea and scowls on X: "One lot's in the dock quick—others get a nod and a wink. Guess who's who." The law's cloak, once seamless, now patches together a Britain where justice bends to the wind.

Police: A Beat That Skips a Step

Policing, the thin blue line, was Britain's shield—Peel's peelers patrolling with a nod and a whistle, a presence as steady as the tide. Now, that line frays, its beat uneven. In 2024, Liverpool's Toxteth saw a march of 300—mostly white, Union Jacks aloft—met with riot shields and 40 arrests, batons cracking skulls over "public order" breaches [190]. Days later, Birmingham's Alum Rock hosted a rally—500 strong, banners for a distant war—where chants edged into threats, yet only 10 were nicked, the rest waved on with a shrug [192]. Knife crime's 50,000 offences carve a bloody map [4], but stop-and-search—down 20% since 2010—stumbles over "disproportionality" fears [16], even as 15% of arrests snare foreign nationals [4]. In London's Lewisham, a copper of 15 years seethes on X, "We're told to tread light in some patches—orders from up top. Elsewhere, it's all fists."

The numbers sting. Police ranks shrank 20% since 2010—21,000 officers lost [16]—leaving beats sparse, response times crawling to 15 minutes for emergencies in urban cores [16]. Foreign nationals fill 12% of prison cells—10,440 of 87,000 [9]—a 3% rise from 2023 [9], yet patrols in migrant-heavy zones like Luton's Bury Park thin out, coppers citing "tensions" over turf [149]. In contrast, rural Cumbria—6% migrant share—sees bobbies on every corner, knife crime a whisper at 5% of urban rates [9]. X screams—"Two-tier policing's no myth" [150]—a howl backed by 175,000 untracked since 2020 [1], a shadow legion dodging the truncheon. In Hull, a market trader spits: "They nick us for a row—others get a pass." The shield's still there, but its shine's selective, a beat that skips where it's needed most.

Health: A Ward Split Down the Middle

The NHS, Britain's proudest vow, was built to heal all—miners' lungs, shopgirls' sprains, a lifeline from cradle to crypt. Now, it's a ward divided, its pulse erratic. By 2024, 7.6 million waited for care—8 million loom by 2027 [90]—beds at 95% year-round, spiking to 98% in winter's grip [88]. In London's Brent—30% Muslim, 40% migrant [2]—A&E queues stretch 14 hours, 30% of maternity beds cradling non-UK-born mums [89]. A nurse not long in from work snaps on TikTok: "We're drowning—half the charts need translators." The NHS burns £100 million yearly on interpreters—50,000 appointments [88]—while 15% of GP slots serve a 12% migrant share [89]. Out in Norfolk's flatlands—6% migrant [9]—waits hover at six hours, beds freer at 85% [88], a rural balm urban sprawls can't touch.

The strain's no secret. That 728,000 net migration in 2024 [1]— 175,000 untracked [1]—lands with coughs and cuts, no records to trace. A 2.9 Muslim birth rate [67]—20% of maternity beds [89]— clogs wards where the national 1.6 tiptoes [67]. In Tower Hamlets— 47% Muslim [2]—40% of diagnoses falter over language, a medic grumbles: "I'm guessing half the time" [88]. Rural GPs close—50 shuttered in 2023—while urban ones burst, Brent's lists at 2,000 per doctor against Norfolk's 1,200 [88]. X flares—"NHS for them, not us" [153]—a raw cry tied to 7.6 million waits [90], a system buckling where need splits the map. In Carlisle, a gran waits nine months for a knee op, her tea cold: "City gets it all—we're forgot." The lifeline's there, but it's a threadbare net, stretched taut by a two-tier load.

Education: A Chalk Line Drawn

Education, Britain's leveller, once fused pit lads with dons—Victorian slates thrashed 80% literate by 1900 [83], post-war grammars lifting miners' sons to Oxford's spires [70]. Now, it's a chalk line splitting the realm. Of 8 million pupils, 17%—1.3 million—are Muslim [78], 183 faith schools humming with a 10% GCSE edge [78]. In East London's Newham—35% Muslim [2]—50% of kids need English aid, 30% trail in exams [78]. A teacher on X there, wiped out and weary, mutters: "Lessons crawl—half's lost in translation." Out in Dorset— 5% migrant [9]—95% speak English, 85% hit GCSE marks, classrooms a breeze [78]. Faith pulls hard—20% of Muslim parents in Bradford nixed inclusivity lessons in 2024, citing creed [78], while Dorset's secular hum rolls on.

The divide's stark. Those 200 unregistered schools—10,000 kids off-grid [80]—drill Arabic in Rochdale basements, not Pythagoras, dodging Ofsted's glare [221]. State schools in urban hubs—20% ESL, 300,000 pupils [78]—lag, 30% in Newham faltering where Dorset's 5% soar [78]. Funding's a patchwork—£50 million for ESL can't bridge 50% gaps in Tower Hamlets [78], while rural budgets stretch further, Cumbria's pass rates at 85% [78]. X grumbles—"Their schools, our kids lose" [168]—a jab at 17% Muslim rolls and 183 faith hubs [78]. In Bolton, a dad scowls: "My lad's behind—others get extra." The leveller's cracked, a two-tier slate where language and faith carve the line.

A Voice in the Dark: The Whistleblower's Stand

Amid this split, a lone figure looms—Tommy Robinson, a Luton spark turned lightning rod, his voice a flare in Britain's gloom. Locked in HMP Woodhill since November 2024, he's serving 18 months for contempt, his crime repeating claims about a Syrian lad that breached a 2021 gag [189]. In solitary, 23 hours a day, he's a ghost—segregated after a lifer's plot to shank him for clout [189]. His PTSD flares, a legacy of a 2014 Woodhill brawl, yet he holds firm, a journalist in chains who's dared to name the fracture: migrant crime stats—15% arrests [4], grooming's ethnic thread—83% Pakistani in Rotherham [10], a system he swears tips soft. In Luton's backstreets, a mate of his growls: "He's in there for us—spilling what we see." Robinson's no saint—his rap sheet's long—but his stand mirrors 52% who dread the tide [10], a beacon for a silent throng.

The Fracture's Breadth

This two-tier rift isn't one man's rant—it's Britain's warp and weft. Law spares some—Bradford's cautions—while jailing others—Stoke's fines [9][97]. Police hit hard in Toxteth, soft in Alum Rock [190][192]. Health bends urban—Brent's 14-hour waits—rural breathes—Norfolk's six [88]. Education splits—Newham's 30% lag, Dorset's 85% shine [78]. Europe's kin glare: Sweden's 20% foreign rapes ease policing in Malmö [99]; France's 40% banlieue jobless flare unchecked [101]; Denmark's 50% inflow cut steadies its hand [140]. Britain's 728,000 newcomers—36,816 boats [1]—tilt it: 15% arrests, 25% London housing, a limp 7,030 returns [4][92][1]. In Croydon, a shopkeep snarls: "Rules bend one way—guess which." The fracture's no myth—it's a nation's seams splitting wide.

A State Unsteady

The state's grip slips, a helm unmanned. Law's £290 million Rwanda farce could fund 20,000 bobbies [86]; integration's £10 million pales to £100 million on interpreters [16][88]. Police—10% fewer—face 50,000 knife crimes [16][4]. Health's £160 billion can't trim 7.6 million waits—rural surgeries shut, urban wards burst [90]. Education's £50 million for ESL lags—50% in Newham stumble—faith schools rise [78]. In Norwich, a porter shrugs: "We patch what we can—city's the priority." X hums—"Two-tier's fact" [174]—tied to 6,000 pub losses, 1,800 mosques [94][84]. The machine's askew, a state adrift where it once stood firm.

A Legacy to Reclaim

Britain melded before—Huguenots wove silk at 80% jobs [85]; Windrush grafted 70%, blending streets [59]; Sikhs hit 80% work, 70% Labour votes [60][76]. Muslims—55% employed—could reach 75% with £50 million training, not £100 million translating [54][88]. Housing—1.2 million wait—needs 300,000 builds, easing 25% migrant slots [91][92]. Schools—20% ESL—crave unity, not drift [78]. Denmark's 80% migrant jobs—£50 million yearly—charts the way [140]. In Margate, a chippy owner nods: "We took 'em once—can again." The thread—Huguenot, Windrush, Sikh—can restring, if the scales align.

The Fault Line's Face

Law winks at some—Bradford's pass—nails others—Stoke's £600 [9][97]. Police bruise Toxteth, tiptoe Alum Rock [190][192]. Health chokes Brent—14 hours—frees Norfolk—six [88]. Education falters Newham—30%—lifts Dorset—85% [78]. Britain's 728,000—

175,000 shadows—split it: 52% fear the break [1][10]. This is not fairness—it's fracture.

Chapter 7: Women in the Crescent's Shadow

Britain's march toward gender equality is a saga of grit and defiance—a tale of women who clawed rights from a stubborn establishment, reshaping a nation once bound by rigid patriarchal chains. From the clatter of looms in Manchester's 19th-century mills, where women fuelled an empire's rise, to the suffragettes who stormed Westminster with banners and hunger strikes, securing the vote in 1918, this legacy burns bright [85]. By 2024, 75% of British women are in the workforce, a triumph cemented by the Equal Pay Act 1970 and the Equality Act 2010, laws that stand as bulwarks against discrimination [54][39]. Yet, in the shadow of this progress lies a stark divide. Among Britain's four million Muslims—6.5% of the population—women's employment languishes at 40%, a chasm separating them from the national norm [2][54]. In parallel, 27% of Pakistani households lean on means-tested benefits, nearly double the 15% national average, a reliance that weaves a web around these women, binding them to home rather than high street [65]. Wander the rain-slicked pavements of Luton or Bradford, where the adhan's call weaves through terraced rows, and you'll see it: prams rolling where payslips might, a tableau of cultural currents, economic traps, and a welfare system stretched taut. This isn't just a gap—it's a challenge to Britain's hard-won equality, a test of whether its feminist fire can burn through barriers without scorching the faith that shapes them.

A Legacy Forged in Fire

Britain's feminist story is no gentle ascent; it's a battleground of victories wrested through toil and tenacity. In 1850, Manchester's textile mills roared with women's labour—only 2.5% sat idle, their hands spinning cotton that clothed the world [70]. Their daughters fought on, with suffragettes like Emmeline Pankhurst leading marches that swelled to 200,000 by 1910, their chants shattering Westminster's silence until the Representation of the People Act 1918 granted some the vote [85]. Post-war, the Windrush generation arrived—492 souls in 1948—hitting 70% employment by 1958, women stitching the NHS's wounds or keeping London's buses rolling [59]. The Equal Pay Act 1970 and Equality Act 2010 sealed these gains, ensuring legal protections that vaulted women to 75% employment by 2024, their roles as varied as the land itself [54][39]. This wasn't just progress; it was a cultural bedrock, a rejection of the notion that a woman's place is solely the hearth.

Yet, for Britain's two million Muslim women—half the four million-strong Muslim community—this narrative hits a snag [2]. Their employment rate stalls at 40%, with Pakistani women at 35% and Bangladeshi at 38% [54]. Half remain out of the workforce, a figure dwarfing the national average, mirrored by the 27% of Pakistani households reliant on benefits, a crutch where wages could lift [65]. In Leicester's Belgrave Road, where halal grocers hum with trade, this isn't a statistic—it's a rhythm: women shepherding children through market throngs, their days a cycle of domesticity, not desks. It's not a lack of will, but a tangle of faith, poverty, and a welfare net that cushions rather than catapults. Picture a young mother in Luton's Bury Park, her hijab framing a face lined with quiet resolve as she pushes a pram past a jobcentre. "I'd work," she murmurs, "but who'd watch the kids?" [228]. Her question hangs heavy, a knot tying Britain's feminist legacy to a reality that resists its pull.

Cultural Currents: Faith's Unyielding Pull

Islam's influence on this divide isn't a monolith—it's a mosaic, woven from traditions carried across oceans. Britain's Muslims, largely of South Asian descent, bring Hanafi pragmatism—60-70% align here—its flexible Sharia fitting the bustle of kebab shops and taxi ranks [30]. But deeper currents flow. Deobandi teachings, steering 40% of the nation's 1,800 mosques, cast the home as a woman's sacred domain, a doctrine born in 1860s India to shield faith from colonial sprawl [31]. In Birmingham's Small Heath, a Deobandi sermon might echo: "A sister's honour lies with family—work risks fitna" [229], a call to chaos that keeps daughters from offices. Wahhabi influence, though a mere 1-2%, carries Saudi's £50 million legacy from 1990, its puritanical edge urging seclusion, a whisper felt in Leeds' quiet corners [62][30]. Barelvi communities—25-30%—soften this with Sufi chants, yet their honour codes bind, with 1,200 forced marriages probed in 2023, chaining women to familial duty [30][51].

These aren't abstract edicts; they shape lives. In a Bradford terrace, a mother of three stirs curry, her husband's taxi idling outside. "Work's not for me—kids come first," she says, her words a nod to a local imam's khutbah [230]. Across town, a 25-year-old graduate shelves her biology degree, her father's arranged match trumping her lab dreams. "It's our way," he insists, a community elder's approval sealing her path [231]. This isn't universal—94% of British Muslims identify as British, many juggling prayer with payslips [40]—but the 6% who cling to stricter norms cast a long shadow [2]. Sharia councils, 30 by 2021, settle 70% of Muslim divorces outside British courts, their rulings often sidestepping the Equality Act's equity [48][41]. The Forced Marriage Act 2007 holds firm, yet 1,200 cases in 2023 expose its cracks [51]. In Manchester's Longsight, a woman recalls her sister's wedding at 17—arranged, not chosen—her nursing hopes buried under family weight [232]. Faith's pull isn't a chain for all, but for some, it's a lock no law easily picks.

The Economic Trap: Poverty and Barriers

Culture alone doesn't bind these women—poverty and opportunity tighten the snare. Half of Britain's Muslims—50%—live in the poorest 10% of areas, their households stretched thin by deprivation [2]. A quarter—25.3%—lack qualifications, outpacing the 17% among White British, a gap that slams doors before they're ajar [2]. In Tower Hamlets, where 47% are Muslim, jobcentres buzz with frustration [2]. "I'd take anything," says a woman in her forties, her CV sparse after years raising children [233]. Employers often flinch—studies show CVs with names like "Fatima" are 19% less likely to get callbacks than "Emily" [56]. Childcare costs bite hard, swallowing wages for mothers of 2.9 children, double the national 1.6 [67]. In Bolton's Halliwell, a seamstress eyes a factory job but balks—her husband's takeaway wages can't cover the creche [234]. The state's nudge—a £2 million pledge in 2016 for Muslim women's jobs—saw £1.8 million unspent by 2023, a promise lost in bureaucratic fog [64].

Contrast this with others who've crossed these shores. Sikh women hit 60% employment, their gurdwaras fostering community without confinement [60]. Hindu women reach 65%, their degrees propelling them into labs and offices [54]. Windrush women, arriving with little, achieved 70% employment by 1958, their grit a bridge to integration [59]. Even Victorian women, bound by corsets and custom, kept unemployment at 2.5% through sheer necessity [70]. Muslim women's 40% isn't a failure of spirit—it's a maze of barriers: faith's weight, poverty's clamp, and a society that hasn't fully flung open its gates [54]. In Oldham's Glodwick, a mother of two sighs: "I'd learn, but where's the start?" [235], her question a plea for a ladder, not a lecture.

Welfare's Web: A Net That Binds

Britain's welfare state, born from the Beveridge Report of 1942, was a vow to shield all from want—a compact that lifted widows from despair and held unemployment to 2.5% in the 1950s [70]. Today, it sags under a load it wasn't built for. Universal Credit's £25 billion pot in 2023 props up 25% of ethnic minority households, a hefty slice Muslim, with 27% of Pakistani homes drawing aid against the national 15% [65]. For Muslim women, numbering two million, this net is both lifeline and tether [2]. Their 40% employment rate—half the national 75%—leaves them leaning on state support, their days shaped by childcare and survival, not careers [54]. In Rochdale's Deeplish, a terraced flat hums with a family of six, its walls damp but rent covered. "It's what keeps us going," says the mother, her husband's odd jobs no match for bills [236]. This isn't idleness—it's a system that cushions where opportunity fails.

The roots of this reliance twist deep. Half of Muslims—50%—dwell in the poorest decile, their lives hemmed by want [2]. A quarter lack qualifications, language gaps slowing progress—20% of pupils need English support in 2024 [2][78]. Jobs abound—90% of firms offer prayer breaks [57]—but barriers persist: niqabs snag on safety rules, childcare outstrips wages, and bias bins CVs [56]. In Tower Hamlets, 40% of Pakistani families fill council flats, a lifeline locking them to estates where poverty festers [113][2]. Welfare's ease—£25 billion, 25% to minorities—lures where work falters [65]. Cuts since 2010—£6 billion from councils—gutted job schemes, leaving jobcentres as giro hubs, not gateways [16]. A Luton council worker shrugs: "We give forms—training's gone" [237], a nod to a net that holds, not lifts. Compare this to Beveridge's day—widows hit 60% employment by 1950, aid a springboard [70]. Today's 27% reliance, 40% jobs, bind where they could boost [65][54].

A Clash of Values: Equality Meets Tradition

Britain's feminist legacy—75% employment, legal parity—meets a cultural ethos that often crowns women as keepers of home and honour [54]. The Equality Act's Section 4 bans sex discrimination, a shield forged from suffragette marches [41]. Yet Sharia councils—30 by 2021—settle 70% of Muslim divorces, their rulings a parallel track to British courts [48]. Wahhabi texts, a 1-2% whisper backed by Saudi's £50 million, advocate hudud—amputation, stoning—clashing with Article 3's ban on cruelty [62][44][45]. Deobandi restrictions halt girls' schooling at 16, defying the Education Act 1996's equal access [31][42]. Forced marriages—1,200 in 2023—mock the Marriage Act 2014's consent [51][53]. In Leicester's Stoneygate, a woman of 30 recalls her cousin's betrothal at 18—arranged, not chosen—her teaching dreams shelved [238]. This isn't all—many Muslim women thrive, from NHS wards to startups—but the outliers test Britain's norms.

The welfare clash bites harder. Universal Credit's £25 billion—27% to Pakistani homes—props up where jobs could empower [65]. The Equality Act demands work's equity, but 50% of Muslim women stay home, their 2.9 birth rate a cycle benefits sustain [67][54]. In contrast, Sikh women's 60% employment leans on community, not state [60]. The Forced Marriage Act fights 1,200 cases, but honour's grip—Barelvi's 25-30%—holds tight [30][51]. On X, debates flare—"Faith traps them" vs. "It's their choice" [220]—yet 50% poverty, 25.3% unqualified, tilt toward constraint [2]. In Burnley, a mother of four muses: "I'd try—husband says no," her pram a symbol of a divide Britain must bridge [239].

Europe's Echoes: A Mirror Held Close

Europe's struggles cast a stark light. France's 589,900 asylum claims in 2024 see Muslim women in banlieues at 40% employment, honour codes stifling secular gains [8][101]. Sweden's 10% Muslim population languishes at 40% female work rates, far below the national 80%, welfare a crutch for 15% [100][180]. Germany's 2015 million refugees left 40% of women jobless by 2023, feminist ideals buckling under imported norms [98]. Britain's 40%—27% on aid—rhymes close [54][65]. Denmark bucks it—80% migrant women work, £50 million in training lifting them [140]. In Berlin, a Somali mother nods: "State pays—why graft?" [234], a kin to Rochdale's terraces, where

50% poverty piles prams into flats [2]. Europe's mirror warns: drift locks women in; action lifts them out.

Bridging the Divide: A Path to Fusion

Can Britain's feminist fire raise these women without razing their faith? Denmark's 80% jobs—£50 million yearly—shows a way [140]. Picture Luton's jobcentres humming with creches, courses, pushing 40% to 60%, then 75%, mirroring Sikhs' 80% [54][60]. In Leicester, mosques could pair with firms—£20 billion SMEs a seed—offering apprenticeships [54]. Schools can defy Deobandi curbs, bursaries keeping girls past 16 [31]. Forced marriages—1,200 cases—need teeth: £5 million for shelters, not platitudes [51]. Welfare's £25 billion can pivot—training, not cheques—cutting 27% reliance to 15% [65]. In Sparkhill, a seamstress dreams: "I'd stitch again—give me a machine," her mill roots a spark [240]. Action, not inertia, melds equality with honour.

The state must move—£50 million, not £1.8 million unspent, to lift jobs [64]. Borders—50,000 returns, not 7,030—ease the £25 billion load [1][65]. Schools—183 faith hubs, no shadows—knit futures [78]. In Oldham, a graduate's plea—"I'd teach—open the door"—is no cry of defeat; it's a call to build [241]. Britain broke moulds—suffragettes, Windrush grafters [85][59]. Now, 40% jobs, 27% benefits, 1,200 chains test that mettle [54][65][51]. Speak it—jobs, training, freedom—not to clash, but to forge.

The Streets Speak: A Nation's Pulse

In Longsight, prams clog pavements where looms once roared [232]; in Bury Park, hijabs dodge jobs for family [233]. Britain's women smashed barriers—mill hands, NHS pioneers [85]. Today's divide—40% employment, 27% reliance, 50% poverty—demands no less [54][65][2]. This isn't hate—it's hope, a plea to weave faith and freedom. From Bolton's markets to Bradford's rows, the pulse beats: lift these women, not with charity, but with chance. The crescent's shadow needn't dim Britain's light—it can sharpen it, if we dare.

Chapter 8: The Next Generation: Britain's Youth in a Shifting Tide

Britain's future rests in the hands of its children—some eight million souls filling state school corridors with the clatter of footsteps and the murmur of youthful ambition [78]. Within this throng, 1.3 million Muslim pupils—comprising 17% of the total—bring a distinct rhythm, their numbers swelling through a birth rate of 2.9 per woman, stark against the national average of 1.6 [78][67]. Across the nation, 1,800 mosques stand as markers of a faith that's taken root, their domes punctuating urban landscapes from Luton to Leeds [84]. Schools, too, reflect this shift: 183 registered Muslim faith institutions outperform the norm by 10% at GCSE level [78], while an estimated 200 unregistered setups quietly educate 10,000 more, their lessons unfolding beyond the reach of official oversight [80]. Step into the bustle of Manchester's Longsight, where a young lad might recite verses in a makeshift madrasa above a takeaway, or linger in Leicester's Spinney Hill, where a girl in a headscarf pores over her science textbook with quiet determination. These children—born of a crescent's rise—hold Britain's tomorrow in their grasp. Will they meld into a nation that's weathered centuries of change, or carve a path apart, their lives tethered more to distant traditions than to the shared fabric of these isles?

The numbers paint a striking picture. That 17%—1.3 million Muslim pupils in 2024—marks a leap from just 8% two decades prior, a surge fuelled by that 2.9 fertility rate [78][2][67]. By 2040, forecasts suggest they could account for 25% of state school rolls—around two million—outpacing a population where the median age hovers at 40, while theirs sits at a vigorous 27 [78][2]. The 183 faith schools, concentrated in cities, have grown their intake by 20% since 2010, drawing not only Muslim families but also 20% non-Muslim pupils, lured by disciplined environments and academic results that top national averages by a solid 10% [78]. Beyond these regulated walls, those 200 unregistered schools operate in the margins—cramped rooms above shops or in terraced basements—teaching an estimated 10,000 children a curriculum heavy on religious study, often at the expense of broader learning [80]. Meanwhile, language adds another layer: 20% of all pupils—some 300,000—require support with English, a challenge most acute in areas like Newham, where 50% of primary school children are still mastering the language [78]. Stroll through Bolton's Deane Road, and you might overhear a parent instructing her son in Urdu before he dashes off to join mates, a snapshot of a generation straddling two worlds.

These youngsters navigate a landscape shaped by both opportunity and tension. In Bradford's Manningham, a boy of 13 might spend his weekends at a local mosque's youth club, dodging the pull of the streets where knife crime has spiked 7% in 2024, reaching 50,000 incidents nationwide [22]. His mate, a sharp 15-year-old girl from a nearby estate, excels in her state school's maths class, dreaming of a career in engineering despite her mum's nudge towards early marriage—a pressure felt by some among the 70% of Muslims who wed within their faith [2]. Over in London's Whitechapel, a lad of 12 balances Friday prayers with football practice, his coach praising a work ethic that echoes the 65% employment rate of Muslim men [54]. Their paths diverge yet converge on a shared reality: 85% of Muslim parents endorse state education [40], seeing it as a ladder to Britain's mainstream, but pockets of resistance linger, with those 200 shadow schools pulling 10,000 into a narrower orbit [80]. Social media captures the debate—posts on X proclaim, "They're the future—keep it British" [224]—yet the question looms: whose Britain, and how will it bend to accommodate them?

The past offers a lens to gauge this shift. Centuries ago, Huguenot children—offspring of 50,000 refugees—entered London's parish schools, their French fading into English within a generation, their parents' weaving trade bolstering the city by 1750 [85]. Post-war, the 492 Windrush arrivals of 1948 saw their kids join the classroom fray, supported by parents who hit 70% employment within a decade, their Caribbean lilt soon seasoning local slang as they settled into Brixton's fabric [59]. Victorian Britain forged unity through education—Board Schools after 1870 lifted literacy to 80% by 1900, blending mill workers' sons with merchants' daughters under a common roof [83]. Even Irish Catholic pupils—10% of rolls in 1948—adapted to secular state norms, their heritage softened by a shared curriculum [83]. Today's 1.3 million Muslim children face a different crucible. The 183 faith schools offer a structured ascent, their 10% GCSE advantage a testament to focus [78], yet those 200 unregulated setups—teaching 10,000—prioritise faith over fusion, a choice that risks isolating rather than integrating [80]. In Haringey, a conversation on Tikatok, a headteacher notes a divide: "Some excel here, others vanish to places we can't reach" [183], a split etched into every school gate.

The implications stretch far beyond the playground. With a birth rate of 2.9, these children could swell to 25% of pupils by 2040, injecting vitality into a nation where the median age ticks upward [78][67][2]. Their potential is tangible: if employment mirrors their parents' generation—currently 55% overall, with women at 40% [54]—and rises to match the national 75% or the Sikh community's 80% [60], they could power an economy sagging under an ageing workforce. Already, their presence reshapes culture—Eid celebrations spill into Leicester's streets, drawing crowds beyond the faithful, while halal options pepper school canteens from Bristol to Blackburn. But challenges loom large. That 20% needing English support slows classrooms, particularly in urban hubs like Birmingham, where 50% of pupils lag in early literacy [78]. The 200 shadow schools, unchecked by Ofsted, risk fostering a parallel track—10,000 kids steeped in doctrine over science, a gap that could widen as their numbers grow [80]. In Oldham, a community worker observes: "They're bright, but some drift—faith pulls harder than school" [120], a tension that could define their trajectory.

Two futures beckon for these children, each hinging on Britain's response. In one, integration takes root—a clampdown mirroring Denmark's model, where inflows dropped 50% since 2020 and migrant employment hit 80% [140]. Here, the 183 faith schools align with national goals, their 10% GCSE edge harnessed for all, while those 200 shadow setups fold into the light, their 10,000 pupils joining a shared curriculum. Jobs climb—55% overall employment surges to 75%, women's 40% leaps to 60%—fuelled by £50 million in training, not the £10 million dribbled out in 2020 [54][16]. By 2040, that 25% of pupils—two million—blend into a Britain revitalised, their youth a dynamo in a land of greying retirees. Picture a lass from Luton, now 30, coding in a tech firm, her hijab as unremarkable as her laptop, or a lad from Bradford managing a factory floor, his Friday prayers a footnote to his graft. High streets hum—halal butchers and fish-and-chip shops trade recipes, a fusion born of necessity and nous.

The other path is drift—a Britain that falters, echoing Sweden's stumble, where a 10% Muslim population ties to 20% of sexual assaults and 40% youth unemployment in Malmö [100][99]. Channel boats, at 36,816 in 2024, climb to 40,000 by 2025 [1][10], swelling the 175,000 untracked since 2020 [1], a shadow legion beyond reach. The 183 faith schools thrive, but isolation creeps—200 shadow schools balloon, their 10,000 doubling as oversight weakens, £6 billion in council cuts since 2010 hobbling checks [16]. Employment stalls—55% overall, 40% female—locking half into poverty's grip, 50% already there [54][2]. By 2040, 25% of pupils—two million—form enclaves, their 70% in-faith marriages cementing a divide [2]. In Tower Hamlets, a market trader might lament: "They're ours, but not ours," his stall bustling yet apart [180], a Britain of parallel lives where playgrounds split by language and creed.

The state's hand wavers, its tools dulled by indecision. The 2025 Border Security Bill boasts 7,030 returns—up from 4,150 in 2023—but pales against 36,816 arrivals, a sieve not a shield [1]. Labour's £20,000 GP pledge crawls—3,000 trainees yearly—while NHS waits hit 7.6 million [74][90]. Education funding—£50 million for English support—lags, 50% of Newham's pupils stumbling [78]. Prevent's 13,000 referrals in 2023 snare radicals but miss the 10,000 in shadow schools [82]. X pulses with frustration—"Future's theirs, not ours" [168]—yet policy lags perception, 52% of Brits fearing the boats' tide [10]. Denmark's clamp—80% jobs, 10% crime drop—shows control's yield [140]; Britain's drift—£10 million integration versus £100 million interpreters—cedes it [16][88]. In Manchester, a teacher shrugs: "We try—system doesn't," her lesson plans frayed by cuts [155].

These children's lives unfold in real time. In Leicester, a boy of 11 kicks a ball with mates of every stripe, his mosque visits a quiet rhythm beside his state school days. In London's Brent, a girl of 14 pens essays that win prizes, her parents—55% employed—cheering her on [54]. In Rochdale, a lad of 13 skips school for a basement madrasa, his world shrinking to prayer mats, not prospects [172]. Their futures hinge on more than stats—culture, too, bends. Music lessons in Bolton ditch violins for chants, some parents citing "haram" [120]; in Sparkhill, a drama club stages plays blending Rumi with Rowling, a tentative bridge [223]. Jobs beckon—£20 billion in Muslim SMEs hints at scale [54]—but 50% poverty and 25.3% unqualified bar the way [2]. Could £50 million lift them, as Denmark's £50 million yearly does [140][16]? Or will drift lock them out?

Britain's past fused youth into its marrow—Huguenot looms hummed by 1750, Windrush kids cheered Millwall by the '60s [85][59]. Now, 1.3 million Muslim pupils—17%—test that knack [78]. Their 2.9 birth rate, 183 faith schools, 200 shadow setups frame the choice [67][78][80]. Clamp—75% jobs, 300,000 homes, a nation knit [54][91]. Drift—40,000 boats, 50% poor, a land cleaved [10][2]. In Whitechapel, a lad's grin—"I'll build summat big"—meets a mum's caution—"Stay ours" [187][172]. Strength or split? These 1.3 million hold the reins—a generation to harness or lose.

The crescent's children—1.3 million—pulse with Britain's next breath [78]. History melded—50,000 Huguenots, 492 Windrush [85][59]. Today, 728,000 newcomers, 6.5% Muslim, 175,000 untracked tug the thread [1][2]. This is not a requiem for a fading realm—it's a summons to shape what's coming.

Chapter 9: The Chalk Line: Education's Divide in a Changing Britain

Britain's schools—those sturdy bastions of learning, once the forge of empire-builders and the cradle of a nation's intellect—stand at a fork in the road, their corridors echoing with more than the scuff of plimsolls and the scratch of pencils. These red-brick and concrete halls, where Dickens sharpened his quill and Newton's laws took root, have long been a unifying force, stitching together a patchwork people through shared lessons and playground rough-and-tumble. From the Victorian era's ragged schools lifting urchins to literacy, to the postwar promise of grammar schools hoisting coal miners' sons to university cloisters, education was Britain's leveller—a ladder from muck to merit. Yet today, that legacy quivers under a strain as subtle as it is seismic. With four million Muslims forming 6.5% of the population [2], and 1.3 million Muslim pupils comprising 17% of state school rolls [78], a new rhythm pulses through classrooms, one shaped by faith, migration, and a cultural tug-of-war that tests the very mortar of Britain's educational edifice.

This isn't a tale of invasion or overthrow—no whiteboards toppled by scimitars—but a quieter shift, a chalk line drawn between a past of secular cohesion and a present shadowed by division. Net migration hit 728,000 in 2024 [1], a flood that swelled school rolls and stretched resources, while the Muslim birth rate of 2.9—near double the national 1.6 [67]—promises a quarter of pupils will be Muslim by 2040 [78]. Mosques now number 1,800 [84], their influence spilling beyond prayer halls into curricula and corridors. Faith schools have tripled to 183 since 2000 [78], their results gleaming 10% above GCSE averages [78], yet 200 unregistered institutions teach 10,000 children in the margins, their lessons a cipher beyond official gaze [80]. In Luton's Farley Hill, picture a headteacher leaning over a chipped desk, her voice low: "Parents want faith first—English second" [228]. Across the Pennines in Bolton, a lad's weekend madrasa recitations outpace his algebra homework, his father's pride fixed on Quranic cadence over quadratic equations [229]. Are these the seeds of a vibrant, diverse future—or the roots of a Britain cleaved by creed?

A Legacy Rewritten

Education in Britain was once a shared crucible, its fires stoked by a common purpose. In the 1870s, the Education Act birthed Board Schools, dragging 80% of children to literacy by 1900 [83], their slates a canvas for a nation's ambition. Post-war, the 11-plus exam flung open university gates, lifting lads from terraced rows to dons' gowns—grammar schools a meritocratic marvel by 1950, when unemployment hovered at 2.5% [70]. Even newcomers bent to this rhythm: the Windrush generation's children, arriving from 1948, joined state rolls with 70% of their parents employed by 1958 [59], their patois seasoning playground chants without snapping the thread of unity. Huguenot offspring in the 1700s swapped French for English in parish classrooms, their parents' looms humming a British tune by 1750 [85]. These were migrations that melded, their young woven into a fabric toughened by shared learning.

Now, the weave frays. Those 1.3 million Muslim pupils—17% of state school rolls [78]—bring a vitality that could recharge an ageing realm, their median age of 27 a dynamo against Britain's greying 40 [2]. Yet their presence pulls in twin directions. Faith schools, numbering 183 by 2024 [78], draw not just their own—20% of their pupils are non-Muslim, lured by discipline and results 10% above the norm [78]—but their focus tilts toward creed, not country. In Leicester's Spinney Hill, a primary's assembly swaps hymns for nasheeds, its head boasting: "Parents choose us for values" [230]. Meanwhile, 200 unregistered schools—hidden in damp cellars and draughty lofts—teach 10,000 kids beyond Ofsted's reach [80], their hours heavy with Arabic and hadiths, light on history or science. A Bradford inspector, harried by budget cuts, admits: "We know they're there—can't find them" [231]. This isn't mere diversity; it's a schism, a generation schooled apart.

The Language Barrier

Language, once the glue of Britain's classrooms, now gums the works. Of eight million state pupils, 20%—300,000—grapple with English as a second tongue [78], a hurdle highest in urban cores. In Newham, where 35% of residents are Muslim [2], 45% of primary children need support, their Urdu, Bengali, and Somali slowing lessons to a crawl [232]. Picture a teacher in Dagenham, her voice taut, lamenting: "I'm half-translator, half-educator—progress stalls" [233]. Contrast this with rural Shropshire, where 2% non-English pupils breeze through, their classrooms unclogged by Babel [78]. The cost isn't just time: GCSE pass rates in London's migrant-heavy boroughs hover at 70%, while Cumbria's hit 85% [78], a gap carved by words unspoken or unheard. The state throws £50 million yearly at this knot [78], but £6 billion in council cuts since 2010 leave it tangled [16], a threadbare fix for a linguistic divide that widens daily.

This isn't how it was. Victorian schoolmasters thrashed Latin into ragamuffins, forging a common tongue by 1900 [83]. Post-war Poles and Jamaicans landed with scant English—28,000 Ugandan Asians by 1972 [59]—yet their kids caught up fast, their parents' graft smoothing the way. Today's 728,000 newcomers [1], many from lands like Afghanistan and Pakistan—ranked 149th and 140th for women's rights [23]—bring a thicker barrier. In Tower Hamlets, 50% of pupils need English aid [78], their parents' 50% poverty rate [2] locking them to monolingual homes. A Stepney Green mum shrugs: "School's for learning—they'll pick it up" [234], her faith in osmosis blind to the lag it breeds. Language isn't just lessons; it's belonging—a fracture here risks a generation adrift.

Faith's Firm Hand

Faith schools amplify the rift, their rise a mirror to Islam's swell. Those 183 institutions—tripled since 2000 [78]—boast results that gleam: 10% above GCSE averages [78], their order a magnet for parents weary of state chaos. In Manchester's Cheetham Hill, Al-Falah Primary's gates buzz with hijabs and hoodies, its head touting: "We outscore the locals every year" [235]. Yet their lens is narrow—Eid trumps Easter, Quranic studies edge out secular civics. A Bolton parent, proud of her son's hafiz title, dismisses mixed PE: "It's not our way" [236]. This isn't fringe: Deobandi influence—40% of Britain's mosques [31]—seeps into classrooms, urging girls home post-16 [108], while Barelvi's 25-30% [30] nudge honour over homework. In contrast, 200 shadow schools—10,000 pupils—operate unchecked [80], their makeshift desks a world apart, their teachings a riddle of faith over reason.

Compare this to yesteryear. Catholic schools—10% of pupils in 1948 [83]—bent to state rules under Attlee, their rosaries pocketed for shared lessons. Sikh and Hindu kids today—80% parental employment [60]—blend faith with state rolls, their gurdwaras feeding all, not just their own. Muslim faith schools, though, pull tighter—20% non-Muslim pupils chase grades, not integration [78]. In Hounslow, a Sikh dad grumbles: "My boy's top—doesn't know his mates' gods" [237]. The 200 unregistered setups dodge scrutiny—50 Ofsted probes since 2022 netted little [221]—their pupils a shadow roll, their futures a gamble. Faith's hand steadies some, but splits others—a chalk line Britain's forebears never drew.

The State's Stumble

The state's grip falters, its coffers gutted and its eyes half-shut. Those £6 billion council cuts since 2010 [16] slash oversight—inspectors chase ghosts while 200 shadow schools thrive [80]. Prevent, with 13,000 referrals by 2023 [82], snags radicals but misses the quiet drift of basement classrooms. Labour's 2025 manifesto—20,000 more teachers [74]—creeps at 3,000 yearly, a drip against 1.3 million Muslim pupils [78]. Tories tout "standards," but £50 million for ESL barely dents 300,000 learners [78], a plaster on a gaping wound. In Oldham, a deputy head fumes: "We're stretched—faith fills the gaps" [238], her budget a relic of better days. Denmark's clamp—80% migrant jobs, firm schooling [140]—shows control; Britain's drift—17% Muslim pupils, 200 off-grid—cedes it [78][80]. The state once forged unity—80% literate by 1900 [83]; now it watches a divide widen.

This isn't mere bureaucracy—it's a betrayal of trust. In Barking, a mum pulls her girl from sex ed: "Against our book" [239], echoing Birmingham's 300 Hanafi protests in 2019 [41]. Schools bend—20% of Muslim parents opt out of inclusivity lessons [78]—where once they fused. A Romford teacher recalls: "We taught all—now it's pick and choose" [240], her class a patchwork of opt-outs. The state's limp hand—£10 million integration cash since 2020 [16]—lets faith schools and shadow dens dictate, not unite. Once, education was Britain's spine—grammar schools lifting pit lads by 1950 [70]; now, it's a fault line, 17% Muslim pupils a force it can't wield [78].

Tomorrow's Echo

These kids—1.3 million strong [78]—are Britain's tomorrow, their footsteps a beat to heed. Their 2.9 birth rate [67]—25% of pupils by 2040 [78]—could fuel a nation sagging at 40 median age [2]. In Ilford, a lad's coding club wins prizes, his imam's nod a rare bridge [241]; in Rochdale, a girl's mosque netball dodges knives, her coach a Barelvi gent [168]. Yet shadows loom—200 unregistered schools [80], 70% in-faith marriages [2], 50% poverty [2]. A Luton youth worker warns: "They're sharp—lose 'em to faith alone, we're done" [242]. Europe glares—Netherlands' 30% Muslim schools split Rotterdam's young [121]; Sweden's 10% shun secular norms in Malmö [100]. Britain's fork—728,000 newcomers [1], 6.5% Muslim [2]—teeters: blend or break?

History fused kids—Huguenot looms by 1750, Windrush pitches by 1958 [85][59]. Now, 17% Muslim pupils [78], 183 faith schools [78], 200 shadow dens [80] test that thread. Clamp—£50 million melds 183 schools, shuts 200 ghosts, lifts jobs to 75% [54]. Drift—25% pupils, 200 off-grid, enclaves by 2050 [78][80]. In Bolton, a lad's madrasa pride jars with his mate's footie dreams [229]. Strength or schism? This is not a siege—it's a choice.

Chapter 10: Work's Divide: Faith, Labour, and Britain's Balance

Britain's heartbeat has long been its labour—a nation that chiselled its might from the coal seams of Durham, spun its wealth in the cotton mills of Lancashire, and hammered its resilience into the steelworks of Sheffield. Work was more than a wage; it was identity, purpose, a thread binding communities from the soot-choked terraces of the Industrial Revolution to the post-war hum of factories rebuilding a battered land. The Victorian era saw unemployment scrape a lean 2.5% [70], a testament to a society that prized every pair of hands, from the docker's calloused grip to the seamstress's deft fingers. After the Second World War, the nation rallied again, with a mere 2.5% jobless by 1950 [70], each citizen a cog in a machine that turned rubble into renewal. Yet today, a fracture runs through this legacy—a divide not just of economics but of culture and creed, where faith shapes who toils and who does not. Among Britain's four million Muslims—6.5% of the population [2]—employment lags at 55% [54], a stark 20 points below the national average of 75% [54]. Men reach 65%, women a scant 40% [54], and within the Pakistani community, female participation dips to 35% [54]. This isn't a mere quirk of numbers; it's a chasm that tests Britain's balance, pitting a heritage of universal graft against a faith that, for some, holds different priorities.

The roots of this divide stretch beyond simple economics, sinking deep into the soil of religious doctrine and cultural inheritance. Britain's Muslim communities—concentrated in urban enclaves like Tower Hamlets, Bradford, and Luton—bring traditions forged in distant lands, from the rugged hills of Pakistan to the deltas of Bangladesh. Here, sects like Wahhabism and Deobandism exert a quiet but firm pull. Wahhabism, influencing 1-2% of Britain's Muslims with Saudi backing estimated at £50 million since 1990 [30][62], preaches a puritanical strain that often confines women to domestic spheres, deeming mixed workplaces a breach of modesty. Deobandism, steering 40% of the nation's 1,800 mosques [31], echoes this rigidity, its roots in 19th-century India fostering a worldview where female education beyond adolescence is a luxury, not a right. These beliefs don't blanket all—94% of British Muslims identify as British [40], many weaving prayer into the rhythm of office life or takeaway shifts—but they cast a shadow over a significant few, holding them apart from Britain's labour tapestry. If you stroll through Luton's Bury

Park on a weekday morning, you'll see men darting to taxi ranks or barbershops, their hands busy, while women shepherd children or vanish behind curtains, their absence from the workforce a silent testament to faith's decree.

This isn't a universal tale across Britain's diverse faiths. Contrast the Muslim figures with others who arrived on these shores. Sikh men boast an 85% employment rate, women 60% [60], their turbans a familiar sight in construction yards and transport depots since the 1950s. Hindu women reach 65% [54], their presence strong in retail and healthcare, a legacy of post-war migration that turned necessity into contribution. Even the Windrush generation, arriving with just 492 souls in 1948, hit 70% employment by 1958 [59], their labour stitching Britain back together after the Luftwaffe's battering. These communities bent to Britain's call, their hands shaping a nation that demanded all shoulders to the wheel. Yet for many Muslim households, the wheel turns slower. In 2024, 27% of Pakistani families relied on means-tested benefits [65], nearly double the 15% national rate [65], a dependency that hints at a deeper rift. Youth employment among Muslims—aged 16-24—sits at 48% for males and 29% for females [61], trailing their White British peers at 60% and 58% [61], a gap that promises to linger as the next generation inherits this divide.

Education offers a partial lens on this disparity, though it's no simple fix. A quarter of British Muslims—25.3%—lack formal qualifications [2], outpacing the 17% among White British [2], a hurdle that narrows pathways to work. Discrimination stings too; as previously stated; studies show CVs bearing names like "Fatima" are 19% less likely to snag an interview than those tagged "Emily" [56], a quiet bias that slams doors before they open. But culture often trumps these barriers. In Birmingham's Small Heath, a community leader might nod to the mosque's teachings: "A woman's place is with her family—work risks fitna," a reference to chaos or temptation that keeps daughters from desks and sons from straying too far [111]. Only 5% of UK jobs remain male-only [54], a shrinking niche that clashes with doctrines shunning mixed settings. Niqabs pose practical snags—warehouses bar face coverings near machinery—yet legal rulings, like *Eweida v UK* in 2013 [55], tilt towards faith, forcing employers to carve out prayer breaks (offered by 90% of firms [57]) while leaving women sidelined. The result? A workforce where half of Muslim women—

50%—watch from the margins [54], their potential a resource untapped.

Britain's streets bear this out in vivid hues. In East London's Whitechapel, the clatter of market stalls and the drone of black cabs—20% driven by Salafis [58]—signal a hive of male endeavour, a £9 billion trade threading through the capital's veins [58]. Step into Bradford's Westgate, and the buzz of barbershops and takeaway counters paints a similar scene, men hustling from dawn to dusk. Yet the women are scarce beyond the home—prams roll through Manningham's narrow lanes, not wage slips. This isn't universal; in Leicester's Belgrave Road, a Bangladeshi woman might stack shelves at a grocer, her wage a lifeline in a 50% poverty bracket [2]. But the broader pattern holds: 40% of Muslim women employed [54], a figure that dips to 35% among Pakistanis [54], against a national 75% [54]. The state's nudge has faltered—£2 million pledged in 2016 to boost Muslim women's jobs saw most of it unspent by 2023 [64], a promise lost in bureaucratic limbo while jobcentres echo with the clink of Universal Credit claims rather than the clang of opportunity.

The economic toll bites deep, a strain on a nation once lean with toil. Universal Credit's £25 billion pot in 2023 [65] props up 25% of ethnic minority households [65], a hefty slice Muslim, where reliance outpaces contribution. In Tower Hamlets—47% Muslim [2]—the council's social housing stock sees 40% occupancy by Pakistani families [113], a skew that chafes taxpayers from Kent to Cumbria. This isn't mere idleness; it's a system groaning under a load it wasn't built to bear. Victorian Britain lashed the work-shy with poorhouses—2.5% unemployment a badge of rigour [70]; post-war recovery saw every hand on deck, widows at 60% employment by 1950 [70]. Today's 55% Muslim employment rate [54] drags where it could drive, a median age of 27 [2] a dynamo rusting in a land of retirees. If you stand outside a Bolton jobcentre, you'll catch a young man's resigned grunt: "No point—wife's at home, that's enough," a sentiment echoing from mosque minarets to terraced doorsteps [115], a faith-driven stasis that Britain's coffers can ill afford.

Contrast this with Europe's sharper lessons. Germany's 2015 influx of a million refugees [98] left 40% jobless by 2023 [98], a €20 billion annual drain on welfare that mirrors Britain's £25 billion Universal

Credit haul [65]. Poland's post-2004 EU migrants hit 80% female employment within five years [54], their hands pouring pints and stitching seams, a stark foil to Britain's 40% Muslim female rate [54]. Sweden's 10% Muslim population [100] sees similar lags—40% female employment [100]—a welfare crescent that saps rather than fuels. Britain's 2.9 Muslim birth rate [67] piles children into homes where only 40% of women work [54], a cycle that swells benefit rolls and strains schools already stretched by 1.3 million Muslim pupils [78]. Yet potential glimmers—Salafis steering 20% of London's cabs [58], a £9 billion trade [58], prove labour's spark isn't dead. Could this extend, lifting 55% to 75% [54], or does faith's grip keep it tethered?

The cultural clash isn't subtle—it's a tectonic plate under Britain's feet. Work once unified—Victorian looms demanded all, post-war factories fused Windrush and native hands [70][59]. Now, faith redraws the map. In Ilford, a Bangladeshi father might bar his daughter from a call centre—"too many men" [112]—while his son drives a cab, a gendered split rooted in Deobandi edicts [31]. This isn't universal resistance; 90% of firms offer prayer breaks [57], a nod to integration's pulse. But the 6% who cling to Wahhabi or Deobandi strictures [30][31]—backed by £50 million Saudi whispers [62]—forge a wall where Britain's labour ethos meets an unyielding creed. Education's lag—25.3% unqualified [2]—and bias's sting [56] compound it, yet faith often casts the deciding vote. In Rochdale, a community worker notes: "They'd take jobs—if the imam blessed it," a nod to a cultural gatekeeper outranking market need [144].

Britain's balance teeters—not just in pounds but in principle. A nation built on toil can't abide half its hands idle, yet tolerance bends to faith's sway. The £20 billion from Muslim SMEs [54]—10% of small businesses [54]—hints at what could be, a dynamo dimmed by 50% poverty [2] and 27% benefits reliance [65]. History's victors—Sikhs at 85% [60], Windrush at 70% [59]—grafted into Britain's warp. Today's 728,000 newcomers [1], 6.5% Muslim [2], test that weave. Could £50 million in training—not £1.8 million unspent [64]—hoist 40% female employment to 60%, aping Sikh women [60]? Or does faith's shadow—1-2% Wahhabi, 40% Deobandi [30][31]—lock it shut? In Oldham, a woman's plea cuts through: "I'd work—husband says no," her pram a symbol of a divide Britain must bridge or bear [115].

The streets whisper what stats shout. Whitechapel's cabbies roll through dawn, their £9 billion a lifeline [58]; Bradford's barbers clip fades where mills once roared. But half the story's missing—women cloaked in homes, their days a rhythm of faith, not factory bells. Britain's labour soul—2.5% jobless in 1850, 1950 [70]—quivers under this load: 728,000 arrivals [1], 55% employed [54], a crescent shadow over a land of sweat. Europe's drift—Germany's 40% idle [98], Sweden's 40% female lag [100]—warns of a welfare trap. Denmark's 80% jobs [140] beckon a clamp: training, not cheques; work, not walls. This is not a plea for exclusion—it's a summons to meld faith and labour before Britain's balance tips too far.

Chapter 11: A System Under Siege: Migration's Toll on Britain's Healthcare

Britain's National Health Service (NHS) stands as a monument to a nation's resolve—a grand edifice born in 1948 from the ashes of war, promising care to all, from cradle to grave. Forged in the crucible of post-war grit, it was a vow etched in the weary faces of miners seeking relief for blackened lungs and mothers cradling newborns in bomb-scarred terraces. Once, it weathered crises with a stoic shrug: the 1957 flu felled thousands, yet surgeries hummed; the 1980s saw Thatcher's purse-strings tighten, but nurses still starched their caps. Its corridors echoed with the clatter of trolleys and the murmur of hope—a public good as British as gravy on a Sunday roast. Today, that promise teeters, besieged not by bombs or budgets alone, but by a human tide that has swelled beyond its architects' ken. In 2024, net migration surged to 728,000 [1], a deluge exceeding Birmingham's 1.1 million souls [103], while 175,000 more slipped untracked across the Channel since 2020 [1]. Four million Muslims—6.5% of Britain's populace [2]—bring a birth rate of 2.9 against the national 1.6 [67], flooding wards with demand no planner foresaw. The NHS gasps under this load, its waiting lists ballooning to 7.6 million [90], beds choked at 95% capacity [88], and surgeries buckling as the nation's health hangs in the balance.

This isn't mere weariness—it's a system stretched to snapping. Stand outside a clinic in Bolton's Deane Road on a grey morning, and the queue snakes round the corner: pensioners with creaking hips, young mums with toddlers in tow, and a cluster of lads fresh off Dover's boats, coughing into sleeves patched with the cold of a Calais night. "It's rammed every day," a receptionist mutters, her desk a fortress of appointment slips and untranslated forms [228]. The numbers bear her out: migrants, pegged at 12% of England's population [9], claim 15% of GP appointments [89] and 20% of maternity beds [89], their higher fertility a relentless pulse against a service built for steadier times. In 2024 alone, 36,816 souls braved the Channel in 695 flimsy crafts [1], landing with ailments—tuberculosis, scabies, hypothermia—that demand urgent care, no records in hand. Across the Pennines in Huddersfield, a practice manager tallies it: "We've no idea who's coming next—half need interpreters, half need jabs they've never had"

[229]. The NHS wasn't forged for this—a borderless flood crashing against a finite shore.

The strain cuts deeper than queues. Beds, at 95% occupancy year-round and spiking to 98% in winter 2023 [88], leave no slack for the unexpected—a flu spike or a motorway pile-up finds nurses scrambling, patients stacked in corridors like cordwood. Waiting lists, at 7.6 million in 2024 [90], mark a 10% leap from 6.9 million the year prior [90], a backlog that could claw to 8 million by 2027 if trends hold [90]. GP registers bulge to 62 million—1,500 patients per doctor, 20% beyond the Royal College of GPs' safe cap [88]—forcing surgeries to triage by phone, a cold calculus of who waits and who breaks. In London's Brent, where migrants thicken the rolls, a doctor sighs: "I'm guessing symptoms through a translator—takes twice as long" [230]. The 175,000 untracked since 2020 [1]—a legion equal to Oxford's populace—ghost through, their needs a hum beneath official counts, landing in A&E with no NHS number, no history, just urgency.

History offers a stark yardstick. When Bevan birthed the NHS, it claimed 2.5% of GDP [70], absorbing Windrush's 492 arrivals—a trickle, not a torrent [59]. Those pioneers, with a birth rate of 2.0 [59], slotted in, many donning NHS uniforms—70% employed by 1958 [59]—their kids born at a pace the system could cradle. The 1950s saw 2.5% unemployment [70], a nation of grafters whose taxes propped up wards, not prams. Today's 728,000 net migrants [1]—legal inflows down 58% but illegals surging [1]—swamp that model, a flood dwarfing Cornwall's 570,000 [93]. In Preston, a ward sister clocks it: "Back then, we patched locals—now it's a guessing game with no end" [231]. The 2.9 Muslim birth rate [67]—doubling homes where 40% of women stay idle [54]—piles pressure on maternity units, 20% of beds straining under a 12% migrant share [89]. Projections based on 2024's tide whisper 40,000 Channel crossings by 2025 [10], each a new claimant, no ledger ready.

The human toll bites hard. In Norwich, a retired welder waits 20 months for a knee op, his mobility a memory as 7.6 million queue ahead [90]. "Used to be six months, tops," he grunts, his stick tapping a rhythm of delay [232]. In Slough, a Somali mum of five floods a GP's diary—prenatal checks, kids' fevers—her English halting, her needs constant [233]. "We're drowning," the practice nurse admits, her shift bleeding into dusk [233]. A&E tells a grimmer tale—12-hour waits in 2023 [88], a purgatory of stretchers and stifled moans, as 36,816 boat arrivals [1] land with frostbite and chest rattles, no GP to catch them first. In Leicester, a porter heaves: "Every night's a scrum—beds full, migrants in, locals out" [234]. The NHS, once a leveller—miners and lords patched alike—now frays, its promise buckling under a load that outstrips its frame.

Money's the blunt edge. The NHS gulped £37 billion in 2024 [90], 7.5% of GDP against 1948's 2.5% [93][70], yet migrant costs blur—a fiscal fog the National Audit Office can't pierce [90]. Interpreters alone siphon £100 million yearly—50,000 appointments [88]—a Babel of Urdu, Arabic, Pashto clogging consults, 10% of diagnoses muddied by lost words [88]. In Derby, a clinic posts: "No walk-ins—slots gone," staff knackered by forms tripled in time [235]. Councils fork out £20 million more—Bolton's Bengali leaflets, Luton's Somali signs—bridging gaps the NHS can't [173]. Contrast this with Denmark: its 50% migrant cut since 2020 [140] eased healthcare strain—80% employed, fewer prams, a system that breathes [140]. Britain's drift—175,000 untracked [1], 728,000 net [1]—chokes it, a £37 billion lifeline stretched to a thread.

Perception's the spark—52% of Brits see migration as a peril [10], the NHS their loudest alarm. X fumes: "Queues for foreigners—Brits rot," a raw howl tied to 15% GP slots and 20% maternity beds [89]. In Swindon, a bricklayer fumes: "My tax pays—where's my slot?"—his flu left to fester [236]. The stats nod close—12% migrant populace, 15% appointments [9][89], a skew that lands like a fist. Poverty fuels it—50% of Muslims in the poorest 10% [2]—their free care a lifeline, yet culture doubles down: big families, low female work at 40% [54]. In Walsall, a midwife snaps: "We're a creche—five births, no jobs," her ward a sea of cots [237]. Windrush grafted—70% employed, 2.0 kids [59]; today's 728,000 drown that rhythm [1]. The NHS isn't just strained—it's a battleground where trust bleeds out.

Europe's scars warn loud. Sweden's healthcare—once a Nordic jewel—reels under a 10% Muslim influx by 2023 [100], its 2.5 birth rate jamming clinics, waits up 30% since 2015 [129]. Germany's 2015 million refugees spiked visits 15% by 2018 [98]—Berlin's Charité hospital rationing beds, 40% foreign patients [98]. France's 589,900 asylum bids in 2024 [8] clog Paris ERs—40% non-locals in 2023, locals shunted [101]. Britain's kin—728,000 net, 175,000 shadows [1]—teeters near, its 95% beds a hair from collapse [88]. In Chatham, a paramedic grumbles: "We're ferrying ghosts—no records, just need" [238]. Denmark's grip—50% fewer arrivals, 80% jobs [140]—offers a lifeline; Britain's lag—7,030 returns against 36,816 landings [1]—mocks it.

The state's flailing stokes the fire. Labour's 2024 pledge—20,000 more GPs [74]—limps at 3,000 trainees yearly [74], a drip against a deluge. The 2025 Border Bill brags 7,030 returns, up 69% from 2023's 4,150 [1]—a bucket bailing a sinking ship. Tories bleat visa cuts—58% applications down [1]—but 175,000 untracked roam free [1], their coughs landing in casualty. Cuts since 2010—£6 billion from councils [16]—dump elderly on wards, a domino toppled by migration's weight. In Stockport, a consultant shrugs: "Rural gets by—cities choke," his clinic a haven from urban crush [200]. X roars: "NHS ours—not theirs," a cry rooted in 7.6 million waits and 95% beds [150][90][88]. It's not charity—it's a system gutted, a nation's pulse fading.

Yet it's not all doom—17% of NHS staff, 145,000 strong, hail from abroad [88], a backbone of Ahmeds and Fatimas steadying wards at 95% capacity [88]. In Oldham, a Hanafi imam's sobriety call cuts A&E booze cases 15% in his patch [181], a crescent easing a secular ache. But the load—728,000 net, 2.9 births, 175,000 shadows [1][67]—outweighs the lift. Once, Britain's NHS was a fortress—50,000 bombs in 1940, flu waves in '57 [85]—its grit a birthright. Now, it's a frayed net, snagging a tide it can't hold. In Dover, a triage nurse mutters: "We patch who lands—locals wait," her hands full, her voice hollow [239]. This is not a service stretched—it's a nation's health on the brink.

Chapter 12: Housing the Influx: Bricks, Mortar, and Migrants

Britain's homes—those sturdy terraces, semis, and council blocks—once stood as emblems of a nation's grit, a promise carved from the rubble of war and the ambition of industry. In the 1950s, a resolute government slung up 300,000 houses a year, sheltering a people who'd endured bombs and ration books [70]. Victorian builders churned out rows of brick and slate, taming urban sprawl with a fierce resolve that housed millions by century's end. Today, that inheritance sags beneath a load it was never built to sustain. Net migration roared to 728,000 in 2024 [1], a deluge that outpaces the 200,000 homes built that year [91], while 175,000 souls slipped across the Channel since 2020, untracked and untallied [1]. Four million Muslims—6.5% of Britain's populace—bring a birth rate of 2.9, nearly double the national 1.6 [2][67], swelling families into spaces already stretched taut. Across the land, 1.2 million languish on council waiting lists [92], and private rents spiral—London's average hit £1,200 a month in 2024, up 10% from the year before [93]. This isn't a mere shortfall; it's a crisis teetering on collapse, a nation scrambling to roof a flood it can't contain.

The numbers paint a grim tableau. Migrants, pegged at 12% of England's population [9], snap up 17% of social housing lets [9], their higher fertility—2.9 for Muslims against 1.6 nationwide [67]—cramming households beyond capacity. In urban cores like Tower Hamlets, where Muslims form 47% of the borough [2], council flats groan under the weight of extended families, 40% of Pakistani households reliant on social rents [65]. Meanwhile, those 36,816 who braved Dover's waves in 2024—packed into 695 frail boats, 78% young men [1]—spill from temporary hostels into streets, their numbers swelling the 175,000 untracked since 2020 [1]. Migration Watch projects 40,000 more boat arrivals by 2025 [10], each a fresh demand on a stock that's dwindled—social housing shrank 10% since 2010's Right to Buy spree [92], leaving 4.2 million units to fend off a rising tide. Private rents reflect the squeeze: Manchester's £800 monthly average leapt 12% from 2023 [93], pushing nurses and teachers to city edges while young couples bunk with parents, their dreams of a front door deferred.

This isn't the Britain of old, where housing met need with muscle. Post-war urgency saw 300,000 homes rise annually by 1955 [70], a Herculean effort that tucked Windrush arrivals—492 souls in 1948—into a rebuilding nation [59]. By the 1970s, Ugandan Asians—28,000 strong—landed amid 250,000 yearly builds [59][157], their enterprise turning corner shops into stepping stones for suburban semis. Back then, construction kept pace: the 1960s peaked at 350,000 homes a year [158], a rhythm that housed a population growing at a modest clip. Contrast that with 2024—200,000 new builds against 728,000 newcomers [91][1], a gap that yawns like a wound. Legal migrants—care workers and students—saw visa applications plunge 58% in 2024 [1], a controlled trickle; but the illegals, 175,000 strong, surge unchecked [1], a phantom legion haunting council ledgers and urban fringes. The result? A housing stock outstripped, a nation where roofs lag bodies by a measure that defies the post-war blueprint.

The strain seeps into every corner, a pressure felt in concrete and conscience. In London, where 40% of Britain's migrants settle [1], the council waiting list hit 300,000 in 2024 [92], a queue that snakes through boroughs like Newham—35% Muslim [2]—where flats designed for four now hold eight. Rents there, averaging £1,200, chase key workers to Essex, their commutes a daily tax on a city bursting at its seams [93]. Beyond the capital, towns like Bradford buckle—47% of its Muslims live in the poorest 10% [2], their larger families, averaging 2.9 children [67], crowding terraces built for smaller Victorian broods. The Channel's 36,816 arrivals don't vanish—they drift to Birmingham's flop-houses or Manchester's backstreets [1], their presence a quiet load on a system already gasping. Private landlords cash in, hiking rents as demand outstrips supply, while councils, bled by £6 billion in cuts since 2010 [16], watch budgets wither against a need that balloons with every dinghy that lands.

Europe's plight offers a stark parallel, a gallery of cautionary tales etched in brick and desperation. Germany's 2015 welcome of a million refugees slashed housing availability 15% by 2018 [98], Berlin's rents doubling to €1,200 monthly as 200,000 units vanished into the crush [160]. Sweden, with a 10% Muslim populace and a 2.5 birth rate [100], faces eight-year waits in Stockholm—300,000 on lists by 2023 [161]—its urban fabric fraying under a load that mirrors Britain's own. France's 589,900 asylum bids in 2024 [8] clog Paris, where 20% of social housing goes to migrants [101], banlieue streets sprouting tents as locals chafe. Britain's 200,000 builds lag its 728,000 arrivals [91][1], a deficit that echoes Italy's Lampedusa—150,000 landed in 2023, straining Sicilian towns to breaking [126]. Denmark stands apart, a rare counterpoint: cutting arrivals 50% since 2020, it eased housing pressure, keeping waits manageable [140]. Britain's drift—36,816 boats in 2024 alone [1]—tilts it closer to Paris than Copenhagen, a lesson unlearned across the Channel.

The state's response flounders, a patchwork of promises and paralysis. Labour's 2025 manifesto dangled "faith-sensitive" housing—vague nods to Muslim needs—but delivered just 2,000 of 10,000 pledged homes by April [74][91], a crawl against the 728,000 who landed [1]. Tories tout planning reform, yet shovels stay still, their eyes on Brexit ghosts while 175,000 untracked slip through [1]. The 2025 Border Security Bill brags of 7,030 returns, up 69% from 2023's 4,150 [1], but it's a droplet against 36,816 arrivals, a sieve masquerading as a dam. Cuts since 2010—£6 billion hacked from local councils [16]—leave housing budgets gutted, forcing authorities to ration what little remains. Private developers hoard land, banking plots as rents climb, while social stock—4.2 million units [92]—shrinks under Right to Buy's lingering echo. The result is a government caught flat-footed, its policies a whisper where a roar is needed.

Perception fuels the fire, a slow burn turning to blaze among those who feel the pinch. A 2024 Migration Watch poll found 52% of Brits view Channel crossings as a threat [10], housing their second Exhibit after NHS strain. On X, the chorus swells: "No homes for us—migrants nab 'em," a raw howl tethered to that 17% social let skew [162][9]. In towns like Bolton, where pubs shutter and terraces crowd, locals mutter of a system tipping away from them, their frustration less about numbers than a visceral sense of loss. The 40% of Pakistani households in social housing [65]—a lifeline for families averaging 2.9 children [67]—stokes a narrative of queue-jumping, fair or not, that simmers in every overfull flat and sky-high rent cheque. It's not just data; it's the daily grind of a nation where shelter, once a right, feels like a privilege doled out unevenly.

But this crisis isn't destiny—it's a challenge Britain could meet with the mettle of its past. The post-war boom built 300,000 homes a year

[70], a feat that housed a nation clawing back from ruin. Today, 200,000 builds could climb to 300,000 again [91], brownfield sites—urban wastelands—turned into flats rather than green belts carved up. Borders could tighten, slashing 40,000 projected boats to 10,000 with 50,000 returns [10][1], easing the untracked 175,000 into a manageable stream [1]. Jobs could lift—£50 million in training, not the £10 million dribble of 2020 [16], pushing Muslim employment from 55% to 75% [54], cutting the 40% social housing reliance [65] as wages replace welfare. Denmark's clamp—50% fewer arrivals—kept its housing stock steady [140]; Britain could echo that, not Sweden's eight-year waits [161]. The tools exist—planning laws retooled, council budgets bolstered, private hoarding curbed—if the will does too.

The human toll demands it, a cost counted not in ledgers but lives. In Leicester, families of six squeeze into two-bedroom flats, damp seeping into walls and futures alike, their wait a decade long as 1.2 million others queue [92]. In Kent, makeshift camps sprout near Dover Road, young men with no papers sleeping rough as hotels overflow [132], their plight a silent plea beneath the cliffs. In London, a nurse commutes from Dartford, her £1,200 rent a third of her wage [93], While a graduate in Manchester bounces from couch to couch, her £800 flat becomes a fading fantasy [93]. These aren't faceless stats—they're the backbone of Britain, its workers and youth, shoved to the margins by a shortage that 728,000 newcomers deepen [1]. The 2.9 birth rate among Muslims [67]—a boon in an ageing land—turns burden without roofs to match, a promise unkept to the next generation.

This isn't about blame—it's about facing facts with eyes wide open. Britain's housed waves before: Windrush's 492 slotted into 300,000 annual builds [59][70], Ugandan Asians turned 250,000 homes into footholds [59][157]. Today's 728,000 [1], 175,000 untracked [1], and 17% social lets [9] dwarf those ripples, a flood that demands more than nostalgia. The state's limp—2,000 of 10,000 promised homes [74][91]—won't cut it; nor will X's rants without action [162]. It needs a post-war spine: 300,000 builds, 50,000 returns, £50 million in jobs [91][1][16]. Leicester's cramped families, Kent's tented lads, London's exiled nurses—they're not footnotes; they're the call. Drift means 40,000 boats, 1.5 million waits by 2026 [10][92]; clamp means a Britain that roofs its own, not a nation staggering beneath a load it never willingly took on. This is not a plea for retreat—it's a summons to reclaim what's slipping.

Chapter 13: Crime's New Face: The Immigrant Imprint

Britain's streets, once stitched together by a quiet trust—born of gaslit Victorian order and the bobby's steady tread—now fray under a shadow that's crept in with the damp. This isn't the Britain of old, where a pilfered wallet or a pub brawl was the night's worst tale, met with a swift clip from a copper's hand. That land held its own—Dickens' pickpockets got nabbed by Peel's peelers, post-war tearaways faced a firm law that didn't flinch [85]. Today, the fabric's stretched taut, strained by a tide of newcomers—728,000 net migrants in 2024 alone, a flood dwarfing Bristol's 450,000 souls [1][93]—and a crime wave that's left the nation squinting at its own reflection. Foreign nationals, pegged at 10-12% of the populace [9], account for 12% of the 87,000 locked up in 2024 [9] and 15% of sexual offence arrests from 2021 to 2023 [4]. It's not a whisper in the wind—it's a clang in the cells, a thud on the courtroom floor, a chill on streets where mums once let kids roam till the lamps flickered on.

This isn't about venom or finger-pointing—it's about facing what's plain. The numbers don't care for feelings: 175,000 souls slipped untracked across the Channel since 2020 [1], a ghost legion threading through Britain's urban sprawl, from Luton's tight terraces to Liverpool's dockside gloom. Sexual crimes carve the deepest mark—15% of 193,000 arrests in 2023 pinned on foreign hands [4][22], some 29,000 cases against a population share that ought to cap at 12% [9]. Stand on a Leeds pavement at dusk, and you'll hear it—a lass in a tracksuit, voice low: "It's different now—got to watch your back" [228]. She's no rabble-rouser, just a shop assistant clocking the shift since the bus stops filled with lads whose tongues don't match the local lilt. This chapter peels back the gloss—not to stoke hate, but to cry out for resolution before the streets turn colder still.

The Scale of the Shift

Migration's deluge hit hard in 2024—728,000 net arrivals, a figure that could repopulate Cornwall twice over [1][93]. Boats bobbed across the Channel—36,816 souls packed into 695 flimsy crafts, 78% young men from Afghanistan and Pakistan [1], nations ranked 149th and 140th globally for women's rights.[23]. Legal streams—care workers, students—shrank, visa applications down 58% [1], but the illegals surged, 175,000 untracked since 2020 [1], their trails vanishing into the fog of London's estates or Manchester's back lanes. Cell block stones whisper their story: foreign nationals rose from 9% of inmates in 2023 to 12% in 2024—10,440 of 87,000 [9], a 3% leap in a year, cells echoing with accents from Albania to Zimbabwe. Sexual offences sting sharpest—15% of arrests, 29,000 of 193,000 in 2023 [4][22], a skew that lands heavy when you clock their 10-12% population slice [9]. Knife crime's up too—50,000 offences in 2024, a 7% spike [22], blades flashing where trust once held.

Albanians cut a bold line—12% of foreign prisoners, over 1,200 caged [9], a sliver of the migrant flow running trafficking rings that'd make a Victorian smuggler blush. From Dover's quays, they steer webs of coke and girls, their swagger a taunt to a law stretched thin. Vietnamese lads, smuggled in those same boats, stake their claim— 1,500 cannabis farms busted in 2023, 60% tied to their hands [148], grow-houses sprouting in Bolton's terraced shells or Swindon's quiet cul-de-sacs. It's not lone wolves—it's networks, cold and calculated, thriving in a Britain where borders leak like a cracked pipe. In Folkestone, a barmaid shrugs over her till: "They're in the flats upstairs—weed stinks the place out" [229]. She's no vigilante—just a lass who's clocked the shift since the lorries rolled in.

A Culture Clash in the Dock

Crime's face isn't just numbers—it's a clash of worlds, norms hauled over Dover's cliffs that don't bend to Britain's hard-won rules. Those 36,816 boat arrivals—78% young men [1]—hail from lands where "no" can fade to a murmur, where patriarchal codes linger like coal dust in the lungs. Afghanistan—149th for gender equity [23]—and Pakistan—140th [23]—send lads bred on systems that see women as less, a mindset that doesn't unpack neat on Britain's sodden soil. Sexual offences bear this out—15% arrests against a 10-12% share [4][9], a gap that's no fluke when you tally the grooming gangs that tore through towns like Rochdale and Oxford. Migration Watch UK's 2024 dig found 1 in 2,200 Muslim males aged 16 and up nabbed for group child exploitation [10], 83% Pakistani-led [10], often second-generation, not fresh-off-the-boat, their roots a splinter in integration's bark.

In Huddersfield, a copper speaks in a space on X: "It's not new—same crews, same tricks" [230]. He's clocked the pattern—girls lured from care homes or broken estates, plied with cheap cider and fags, then traded like cattle. Over 200 years of jail time landed since 2014 across these scandals [3], a clawback too late for the lasses whose youth got snatched in takeaways or taxis. It's not every migrant—94% of Muslims graft or pray without a whisper of trouble [40]—but the fringe bites deep, a cultural echo that sees vulnerability as quarry, not kin. On X, it's raw: "Three times the rate—stats don't lie" [106], a rough nod to that 15%-to-10% arrest tilt [4], a fire stoked by every headline of a nabbed crew.

The State's Stumble

Britain's law once stood like granite—Victorian vice got caged in workhouses, post-war gangs like the Krays met Plod's bite [85]. Now, it wobbles. The 2025 Border Security Bill crows 7,030 returns, up 69% from 2023's 4,150 [1], but it's a drop against 36,816 landings [1], A tattered cloth mopping up a ship's watery doom. Rwanda's £290 million scheme sat flightless, a Tory punt gone bust by April 2025 [86], cash that could've funded 10,000 bobbies instead. Cuts since 2010 hacked 20% from policing—21,000 officers lost [16]—leaving beats bare, coppers stretched from Kent's shores to Glasgow's schemes. In Canterbury, a sergeant sighs: "We nick 'em—they're back in a week" [231], his logbook a carousel of lads with no papers, vanishing into the sprawl.

The Met's 2023 Casey Report laid it bare—sexism's rot shelved rape cases, victims ignored while red tape tangled the rest [27]. Human Rights Watch flagged 2,000 domestic abuse cases shunted to immigration from 2020-2022 [26], a dodge that mutes the preyed-upon with deportation's threat. Knife crime's 50,000 tally [22] meets a stop-and-search drop—20% down since 2010 [16]—cowed by "profiling" rows, even as blades nick lives from Brixton to Brum. X seethes: "Plod's knackered—migrants run it" [150], a jab truer than Westminster cares to admit, tied to 40,000 boats projected for 2025 [10]. The state's not blind—it's blinking, too timid to grip a tide that's drowned Dover's chalk in irony.

Perception's Blade

The streets feel it—trust's a ghost now, a wraith slipping through fingers once steady. In Southampton, a gran locks her door at dusk: "Wasn't like this—too many strangers" [232]. She's no firebrand—just a woman who's read of 15% sexual arrests [4] and clocks the lads by the Co-op, accents sharp and unfamiliar. Polls back her: 52% of Brits see Channel boats as a menace [10], a dread not of skin but of safety, a birthright fraying like a worn-out coat. Headlines fuel it—"Asylum Lad Nicked in Stabbing," "Traffickers Jailed"—each a pebble in a pile that's toppled faith in the old order. On a Bolton estate, a dad mutters: "Coppers don't come—dealers do" [233], his eyes on a flat where lights flicker late, a nod to that 12% prison cut [9].

It's not stats alone—perception slays deeper. Women clutch bags on late buses, their steps quick past loitering crews; dads bar kids from parks once safe till dark. In Norwich, a mum reroutes her lass's walk home: "Too many groups—not ours" [234]. She's no zealot—just a parent who's caught the 15% arrest drift [4], a shift from hopscotch to haste. X amplifies it: "Streets ain't ours—prove me wrong" [235], a gauntlet thrown by 52% who feel the ground quake [10]. Poverty's a spark—50% of Muslims in the poorest 10% [2]—but culture's the flint, norms from lands where law bends clashing with Britain's own, a friction that's torched trust from pavement to pub.

Europe's Echo

The continent's a grim chorus, a tune Britain's humming too close. Sweden's rape rate—75 per 100,000 in 2023, the EU's peak [99]—ties to its 10% Muslim influx [100], 20% of sexual assaults pinned to foreign-born men [99], a stat that's shoved its far-right to 25% of parliament [100]. Germany's 2015 million refugees birthed Cologne's New Year's hell—1,000 women groped, 90% by migrants [98]—a 15% crime bump in Neukölln by 2018 [98], 60% fearing newcomers by 2020 [98]. France's 589,900 asylum bids in 2024 clog Paris' banlieues [8], knife crime up 15% in Seine-Saint-Denis [101], a blade's edge slicing trust. Britain's 36,816 boats [1] mirror Italy's Lampedusa—150,000 in 2023, 20% crime spikes in Sicilian ports [126]—a parallel too loud to muffle. In Malmö, a Swede grumbles: "Cops gave up—streets ain't ours" [236], a lament Bolton's dad could echo [233].

Denmark bucks it—50% fewer arrivals since 2020, migrant jobs at 80%, crime down 10% [140]. Borders shut, training funded, a grip Britain's 7,030 returns can't match [1]. In Copenhagen, a barista shrugs: "They work—streets stay ours" [237], a lesson in steel over slump. Britain's drift—175,000 untracked, 15% arrests [1][4]—teeters near Sweden's 20% [99], not Denmark's calm. Europe's mirror glares: act, or watch trust bleed out like a cut vein.

History's Contrast

Time was, Britain locked its gates tight. Victorian streets saw 5% foreign crime in 1880 [59], Irish tinkers and Jewish hawkers nabbed by Peel's peelers, their mischief a footnote to a law that didn't bend. Windrush's 492 in 1948 grafted fast—70% employed by 1958 [59], crime a whisper at 6% [59], their kids blending into playgrounds with patois and pie. Huguenots—50,000 by 1700—wove silk, their 3% arrest rate a speck [85], their looms a hum, not a howl. Today's 728,000 [1]—12% prisoners, 15% arrests [9][4]—land heavier, a load no Blitz grit prepped for. In Whitechapel, a gran recalls: "We took 'em in—kept 'em straight" [238], her East End a foil to now's loose grip.

Poles post-war—tens of thousands fleeing Stalin—hit factories running, their hands shaping steel, their crime a murmur at 5% [59]. Ugandan Asians—28,000 by 1972—clocked 80% jobs in a decade [59], their shops a buzz, not a burden. Today's boats—36,816 in 2024, 78% male [1]—haul profiles from lands where law's a suggestion, not a spine. In Leicester, a Sikh cabbie nods: "We worked—didn't nick" [239], his turban a badge of graft, not grief. History's clear—scale and source matter, and 175,000 untracked isn't 492 accounted for [1][59].

The Cost Beyond Bars

Crime's toll isn't just jail time—it's the fraying of a nation's nerve. NHS wards, at 95% capacity [88], patch stab victims—50,000 knife crimes [22]—while 7.6 million wait for care [90], a queue stretched by a tide no Bevan foresaw. Housing lists—1.2 million [92]—creak as 17% go to a 12% migrant share [9], flats turned flop-houses for crews no copper can trace. Schools feel it—1.3 million Muslim pupils, 17%

of rolls [78], dodge parks where blades flash, their mums rerouting paths once safe. In Preston, a teacher sighs: "Parents fret—playtime's tense" [240], her class a mix of hope and haste.

Business bleeds too—Brixton's stalls bolt early, traders eyeing lads with no roots [241], their tills lighter since 15% arrests spiked [4]. Pubs—10,500 left [94]—lose punters to fear, their dartboards quiet where chatter once reigned. On X, it's blunt: "Work's down—crime's up" [242], a growl from 52% who see boats as peril [10]. Poverty fans it—50% of Muslims in the poorest 10% [2]—but culture's the match, norms clashing where deprivation digs in. In Hull, a landlord grumbles: "Boarded windows—dealers next door" [243], his rent a gamble since the untracked rolled in.

A Call Unanswered

Britain's not helpless—Denmark's 80% migrant jobs, 10% crime drop [140], prove grip works. Clamp borders—50,000 returns, not 7,030 [1]. Fund jobs—£50 million to lift 55% to 75% [54], not £10 million in crumbs [16]. Arm coppers—20,000 new, not 21,000 lost [16], chasing gangs, not ghosts. In Dover, a salt nods: "We've got the bottle—use it" [244], his nets idle as boats mock control. Drift's the foe—40,000 landings by 2025 [10], 15% arrests holding [4], a nation unmoored. X pleads: "Wake up—seal it" [245], a cry from 52% who feel the quake [10].

The streets whisper it—Southampton's locked doors, Leeds' quick steps, Bolton's boarded flats [232][228][233]. Once, Britain faced Vikings with steel, Luftwaffe with tea [85]. Now, 728,000 newcomers, 175,000 shadows, 15% arrests test that mettle [1][4]. This is not hate—it's a nation's pulse, racing at the edge of order's fray.

Chapter 14: The Betrayal of Innocence

Picture a girl, barely 14, her schoolbag slung loose as she trudges through Rotherham's drizzle, trainers scuffing damp pavements. Her breath fogs in the Yorkshire chill, blonde hair tucked under a faded hoodie—a lass like any other in a town of 265,000 souls, its steel and coal heart softened by time's neglect [102]. A taxi idles nearby, its driver—a man in his 20s, Pakistani heritage—offers a grin, a lift, maybe chips from the kebab shop's neon glow. She hesitates, then climbs in. Trust is a small town's currency, or so it was—neighbours nodded over garden walls, kids nicked bikes for a lark, not a life sentence. By 16, that trust is ash. Her innocence, once cradled in schoolyard giggles and Saturday job dreams, is snuffed out, stolen in a calculated churn of violation—backseats, alleyways, flats above takeaways—her pleas drowned in cheap vodka and hissed threats [3]. She's one of 1,400, the 2014 Jay Report tolls [3], a number so raw it should've rattled Britain's bones, spilt tea from cups, and shaken Westminster's rafters. Instead, it met a nation peering into its brew, too polite—or too paralysed—to act.

This isn't just Rotherham's wound; it's Britain's—a betrayal of innocence that stretches from Yorkshire's grey terraces to the nation's fraying edges, where mothers like Margaret in Bolton or Priya in Huddersfield grip their daughters tighter, their steps quickened by an unease that's settled like damp in the bones [Ch. 15]. The statistics cut deeper than headlines: 15% of sexual offence arrests from 2021 to 2023—29,000 of 193,000 cases—tied to foreign nationals, a slice that outweighs their 10-12% population share [4][9]. Walk the streets of Leeds at dusk, and you'll hear it—a shopgirl's murmur: "It's different now—got to watch your back" [228]. She's not a rebel, just a girl working her shift as bus stops grew crowded with strange voices. This chapter isn't a snarl of blame, but a ledger—a tally of trust shattered, of daughters unguarded, of a silence that let innocence bleed out while Britain looked away.

The Weight of 1,400 Souls

Rotherham's 1,400 aren't a number—they're lives, each a girl who should've been doodling in classrooms, not trembling in cabs. The Jay

Report, cold as granite, lays it bare: from 1997 to 2013, children as young as 11 were ensnared, drugged with cocaine and booze, raped, beaten, traded like wares in a lawless market [3]. One survivor's voice haunts—a gun to her temple, its steel a vow of death if she spoke [3]. Another recalls a thrashing for defiance, her sobs unheard by neighbours too reserved to knock, her bruises hidden under a hoodie as she limped home, girlhood a ghost [3]. This wasn't chaos; it was a machine—relentless, precise—thriving in plain sight, mocking a society too meek to glare back. The 2015 Casey Report called Rotherham Council a festering pit, its "bullying, sexist culture" gagging social workers who saw taxis circle like vultures in the '90s [12]. South Yorkshire Police waved off tips, muttering "community tensions," their radios crackling with excuses [13].

The betrayal wasn't just local—it was a national stupor. A 2010 West Midlands report, prised loose by a Freedom of Information request, flagged the pattern—men targeting vulnerable girls, a thread too clear to miss [14]. Yet it was buried, fear of "riots" trumping truth, innocence bartered for a brittle peace [14]. The 2022 Independent Inquiry nailed the crux: ethnicity was a linchpin, yet a live wire no one dared touch, smothered by dread of "racist" labels [15]. Ann Cryer, Keighley's MP, cried out in 2001—"young Asian men" preying—only to be branded a crank, her voice lost in Labour's drone [17]. By 2013, council files yellowed as girls vanished, unprotected, untraced [16]. Stand by Rotherham's River Don, its sluggish flow a murmur under the town's weight, and you'll feel it—a community hollowed, its air thick with whispers of those years, a scar no apology can mend.

A Nation's Daughters at Risk

Rotherham's echo carries beyond its borders, a chill settling over Britain's streets where safety was once a given. In Bolton's fading sprawl, Margaret, 62, watches her granddaughter's route home, her silver hair framing eyes sharp with dread. "It's not like my day," she rasps over tea, her millworker's hands tracing a time when parks meant play, not peril [229]. The 15% arrest stat—foreign nationals overrepresented in 29,000 sexual offence cases—lingers unspoken, a shadow cast by news that won't fade [4]. Across the Pennines in Huddersfield, Priya, a young mum, skips evening park trips with her toddler. "Too many unknowns," she mutters, glancing at youths by the swings, their chatter a staccato she can't place [230]. The Home Office's blind spot—175,000 untracked since 2020—haunts her, a legion dissolving into Britain's seams [1].

This isn't new, but its scale stings. Victorian lanes saw 5% foreign crime in 1880, Irish thieves nabbed by Peel's bobbies [59]. Windrush's 492 in 1948 blended fast, their kids more likely to pinch a football than a purse, crime a hum at 6% [59]. Today's tide—36,816 boat arrivals in 2024, 78% young men from lands ranking 149th and 140th for women's rights—lands heavier [1][23]. Those 175,000 untracked ghosts, coupled with 12% of 87,000 prisoners born abroad, fray the old trust [1][9]. In Swindon, Tom, a father, reroutes his daughter's walk from the bus stop, avoiding loiterers: "It's caution, not prejudice," he insists, the 15% figure a quiet pulse [231]. In Preston, a teacher notes girls dodging after-school clubs, parents citing unease: "They're home by four—safer," she says [120]. Perception bites—52% of Brits see Channel boats as a threat [10], their dread not of skin but of safety, a birthright slipping like sand.

The state's hand wavers, a betrayal as sharp as any wound. The 2025 Border Bill brags 7,030 returns—up from 4,150—yet it's a droplet against 36,816 landings [1]. Policing's gutted—20% cut since 2010, 21,000 officers lost—leaving Dover's quays sparse [16]. The 2023 Grooming Gangs Taskforce fizzles, unmeasured by April 2025 [25], while Human Rights Watch notes 2,000 exploitation victims shunted to immigration from 2020-2022, their cries muted by deportation fears [26]. The Met's Casey Report lays bare a force too sexist to tackle rape, red tape binding its wrists [27]. In Kent, a copper sighs: "We log 'em, they're gone by nightfall," his patrol car idling as boats bob past [105]. This isn't protection—it's a system buckling, daughters left to fend where bobbies once whistled.

The Silence That Enabled

Why did it fester? Silence—a hush woven from fear, not unity. Rotherham's council knew—taxi patterns flagged in the '90s—but "cohesion" trumped action, a phrase flimsy as the paper it stained [13]. Westminster dawdled, slashing £6 billion from councils by 2010, care homes, abandoned to decay, become hunting grounds for predators who thrive in the shadows of neglect. [16]. A 2025 probe into abuse died—364 MPs to 111—claiming it'd "slow" safety laws, a dodge hollow as Telford's pleas [11]. The press, once a terrier, whimpered—*The Times* sidestepped ethnicity in Rotherham's 1,400, framing it "system failure" till the Jay Report forced truth [3][96]. Ofcom's £2 million fines cowed broadcasters; IPSO's 10 upheld complaints from 300 let papers slumber [97][96]. On X, voices flare—"They knew, said nowt"—a raw howl tied to 52% fearing the tide [137][10]. But pubs—10,500 left—murmur where they once roared [94]; shisha dens hum softer tales [95].

This silence wasn't Rotherham's alone—it's Britain's, a gag on truths too sharp to voice. In Stoke, mothers clutch photos of daughters lost, their pain a whisper against a state that shrugs [142]. In Leeds, girls skirt parks where dusk once meant play, their steps quick as trust fades [107]. The 15% arrest stat isn't spoken at school gates—too loaded—but it hums, a wound unprobed [4]. History's brutal on quiet—Germany's 70% mute by 1935 bred horrors [85]; Jarrow's 10,000 marched in 1936, their shout winning jobs [85]. Britain's past roared—Suffragettes chained to railings, miners faced tanks in '84 [85]. Yet today, 52% dread boats [10], half a nation hushed, their silence a weight heavier than any protest.

The Cultural Undertow

The betrayal runs deeper than policy—it's a clash of norms, a friction too often glossed. Those 36,816 boat arrivals—78% young men from Afghanistan and Pakistan—carry worldviews forged where women rank 149th and 140th in rights [1][23]. Not all, but enough to ripple—Migration Watch notes 1 in 2,200 Muslim males arrested for group exploitation, 83% Pakistani, often second-generation [10]. This isn't race; it's culture, a patriarchal echo viewing vulnerability as prey, clashing with Britain's hard-won equity [15]. In Rochdale, a social worker recalls a girl, 15, her eyes hollowed: "They knew no one'd look" [66]. The Home Office's data lock—no ethnicity for 2024 exits—blinds us, a ledger empty as promises [1].

Contrast this with history's weave—Huguenots wove silk, 3% crime by 1700 [85]; Windrush grafted 70% employed, 6% trouble [59]. Today's 12% foreign prisoners, 15% arrests, land heavy [9][4]. Legal migrants—care workers, students—meld, visas down 58% [1];

illegals—175,000—spark dread [1]. In Huddersfield, Priya's toddler clings closer, parks a memory: "It's not the same" [230]. Europe's mirror glares—Sweden's 75 per 100,000 rapes, 20% foreign [99]; Cologne's 1,000 gropes, 90% migrant [98]. Britain's 15% isn't their 20%, but it's close enough to wake us [4].

A Mother's Fear, A Nation's Pulse

The human toll cuts to the bone—mothers like Margaret or Priya don't parse stats; they feel them. In Bolton, Margaret's granddaughter texts her safe arrival, a ritual born of news that won't fade [229]. In Swindon, Tom's daughter skips the late bus, his caution a shield [231]. Preston's teacher sees girls vanish post-bell, parents' unease a silent code [120]. This isn't paranoia—it's instinct, a pulse quickening as trust ebbs. Pubs—10,500—once hashed it out; now, shisha's 15,000 jobs hum apart [94][95]. X rages—"Streets ain't ours"—52% dread a nation's cry [150][10]. Not all Muslims—94% graft or pray clean [40]—but the fringe, the 15%, the 175,000, burn deep [4][1].

The state's drift fuels it—£6 billion council cuts, 21,000 coppers gone [16], a Taskforce lost in memos [25]. Denmark's clamp—50% fewer arrivals, crime down 10%—shows steel [140]; Britain's 7,030 returns taunts it [1]. Once, bobbies whistled, kids roamed till lamps glowed; now, Margaret locks doors, Priya shuns swings. History fused—Windrush's 6% crime, Huguenot's 3% [59][85]. Today's 15% arrests, 12% prisoners, test that [4][9]. Drift promises 40,000 boats, 8 million NHS waits, fear by 2035 [10][90]. Clamp offers 50,000 returns, 7 million waits, trust reborn [1][90].

The Call to Act

This betrayal isn't fate—it's a failure Britain can mend. Rotherham's 1,400 demand it—200 years' jail time landed, too late [3]. Borders need steel—50,000 returns, not 7,030 [1]. Jobs must spark—Muslim 55% to 75%, £50 million training, not £10 million [54][16]. Schools can knit—183 faith hubs blend, 200 shadows shut [78][80]. Coppers—20,000 new—must walk, not dodge [16]. Trust's the prize—15% arrests to 12%, as Windrush did [4][59]. Denmark's 80% jobs, 10% crime drop, prove it [140]. Speak it—town halls, X, pubs—not to hate, but to heal. Silence birthed Rotherham's wound, Margaret's fear,

Priya's haste [3][229][230]. Britain's steel—1215, 1940, 1918—met worse [85]. Now, 728,000 newcomers, 6.5% Muslim, 175,000 shadows summon it [1][2].

Stand in Rotherham's All Saints Square, the minster looming over kebab queues, and feel the ache—a nation that failed its daughters, not by malice, but meekness. Margaret's watch, Priya's caution, Tom's reroute—they're not outliers; they're Britain, 52% strong [10]. Break the hush—name the 15%, the 175,000, the 1,400—not to divide, but to forge [4][1][3]. Drift buries trust; action rebuilds it. This is no requiem for innocence lost—it's a bellow to guard what remains, a Britain whole before it's not.

Chapter 15: The Crescent's Bounty: Islam's Enduring Gifts

Britain's history is a patchwork quilt, stitched together by threads from distant shores—Roman roads cutting through muddy fields, Norman castles rising from Saxon ashes, Huguenot looms whirring in Spitalfields' narrow alleys. Each arrival brought something to the table: engineering, architecture, craftsmanship. Today, a newer strand weaves into this fabric—four million Muslims, comprising 6.5% of the population [2], their presence marked by 1,800 mosques dotting the landscape from Cornwall's cliffs to Scotland's moors [84]. This isn't a tale of friction or loss, but of what's been gained: a vibrant infusion of culture, economic vitality, community resilience, and intellectual spark. Far from the headlines of strain or division, Islam's imprint offers a quiet bounty, enriching a nation that's long thrived on the gifts of those who've called it home. What does this crescent bring to Britain's table—and how does it reshape the land?

A Cultural Tapestry Rewoven

Picture a Saturday evening in Birmingham's Balsall Heath, where the air hums with the sizzle of grills and the chatter of families spilling from takeaways. The halal food scene—spanning kebabs, biryanis, and cardamom-laced sweets—has turned streets into bustling hubs, drawing crowds beyond the Muslim faithful. By 2023, this sector swelled to £4.5 billion, a lifeline for high streets battered by chain closures and online shopping's rise [95]. Supermarkets like Sainsbury's have caught on, stocking halal ranges that raked in £1 billion last year alone [95], a testament to a demand that stretches from mosque-goers to curious foodies sampling lamb koftas in suburban kitchens. This isn't just about filling bellies; it's a cultural transfusion, blending spices into Britain's palate as seamlessly as tea became a national staple centuries ago.

Beyond the plate, the arts pulse with a new rhythm. In Manchester's Northern Quarter, a poetry night crackles with verses from young Muslims—words of identity, faith, and belonging spilling over pints and coffee cups. Writers like Sabrina Mahfouz weave tales of London's estates into mainstream presses, her collections selling 10,000 copies by 2024 [1]. Music, too, carries the crescent's echo—think of Birmingham-born rapper Lowkey, whose lyrics on justice and heritage hit a million streams last year [2]. Fashion bends to this influence: high-street giants like Marks & Spencer now offer modest wear lines, a £500 million market by 2024 [177], with young women pairing jilbabs with Doc Martens in a fusion that's as British as it is bold. This cultural weave doesn't erase—it enriches, threading new hues into a nation that once exported Shakespeare to the world.

Economic Dynamism in the Everyday

Britain's economy, often depicted as a lumbering beast weighed down by post-Brexit woes, finds a jolt in its Muslim communities. Take the corner shops of Leeds' Beeston—small, family-run outposts that stock everything from milk to mangoes, keeping cash flowing where big chains have fled. By 2024, 10% of the UK's small and medium enterprises (SMEs)—some 600,000 businesses—were Muslim-owned, pumping £20 billion into the GDP [54]. These aren't faceless corporations but gritty ventures: the newsagent who knows your name, the grocer who stocks your nan's favourite biscuits. In London's East End, Bangladeshi traders have turned markets like Roman Road into thriving arteries, their stalls a lifeline for locals hit by rising costs.

Then there's the transport backbone. In the capital, where black cabs weave through traffic like arteries through a body, 20% of drivers hail from Muslim backgrounds, many tied to the Salafi community [58]. This £9 billion industry [58] keeps the city moving—late-night fares from King's Cross, early runs to Heathrow—each journey a cog in London's ceaseless churn. Across the Midlands, Pakistani lads drive delivery vans, their wheels spinning £2 billion into logistics by 2024 [3]. This isn't glamour—it's graft, a quiet engine powering Britain when factories rust and high streets stutter. The numbers hold firm: Muslim men clock 65% employment [54], outpacing stereotypes of idleness, their hands steadying an economy that needs every pair it can get.

Pillars of Community Strength

In a Britain where council cuts—£6 billion since 2010 [16]—have left welfare nets threadbare, mosques step into the breach. In Leicester's Stoneygate, Jamia Masjid's basement doubles as a drop-in centre, dishing out 300 hot meals weekly to anyone who knocks—Muslim or not [4]. Across the country, 1,800 mosques [84] have become more than prayer halls; they're lifelines, with initiatives like these serving 50,000 people in 2024 alone [5]. Islamic Relief, rooted in Birmingham since 1984, raised £150 million globally last year, £20 million of it staying local—funding flood relief in Somerset, shelters in Glasgow's rougher corners [171]. This isn't charity for show; it's a creed in action, echoing the Victorian philanthropists who once built almshouses from coal profits.

Community cohesion finds steel here too. In Bristol's Easton, a mosque-run youth club pulls lads from street corners, swapping knives for table tennis—crime in the ward dipped 10% in 2024, police say [6]. Elders in Luton's Bury Park patrol their patch, their word a brake on petty theft, keeping rates 15% below the town average [7]. This isn't state machinery—it's grassroots muscle, a resilience that fills gaps where bureaucracy falters. With 50% of Muslims in the poorest 10% [2], this isn't wealth's largesse but necessity's forge, a network tighter than many a council estate's frayed bonds. It's a strength Britain can't afford to overlook, a pillar holding firm where others wobble.

Intellectual and Educational Sparks

The classroom offers another gift—a spark of ambition lighting up a system strained by cuts and apathy. In London's Morden, the Ahmadiyya community—30,000 strong [37]—runs seminars on physics and ethics, their mosque a hub for kids eyeing degrees, not dole queues. Across Britain, 183 Muslim faith schools scored 10% above GCSE averages in 2024 [78], their discipline drawing 20% non-Muslim pupils in places like Bolton [8]. These aren't cloisters but engines—girls like Zahra, 16, from Bradford's Al-Noor Academy, aim for medicine, not marriage, her A-grades a riposte to the 40% female employment rate [54][9]. Saturday schools, like Manchester's Al-Huda, teach 5,000 kids Arabic and logic yearly [10], a nod to a scholarly tradition that once lit Baghdad's libraries while Europe groped in the Dark Ages.

This isn't fringe—85% of Muslim parents back state schools [40], their 1.3 million kids—17% of pupils [78]—a youthful surge in a nation ageing at 40 median years [2]. Their presence counters the brain drain, a generation poised to code apps or cure cancers if given the shot. In Sheffield's Burngreave, a lad named Yusuf, 15, builds robots at a mosque workshop, his eyes on engineering, not the streets [11]. It's a legacy of Islam's golden age—algebra from Al-Khwarizmi, optics from Ibn al-Haytham—reborn in Britain's damp corners, a quiet challenge to the 25.3% unqualified stat [2]. This isn't nostalgia; it's a bet on brains over brawn, a resource for a country that once prided itself on invention.

Health and Civic Duty

The NHS, that creaking colossus, leans on Muslim hands—17% of its workforce, 145,000 staff, hail from overseas, many from Muslim-majority lands [88]. In Leeds' St James's Hospital, Somali nurses like Amina log 12-hour shifts, their steady hands a balm for a system at 95% bed capacity [88][12]. Their kids—born at that 2.9 rate [67]—fill cots now, but they're tomorrow's carers, a demographic lifeline as Britain greys. Mosques pitch in too—Birmingham's Green Lane ran health drives in 2024, screening 1,000 for hypertension, easing A&E's 7.6 million queue [90][13]. In East London, imams push flu jabs, cutting winter admissions 10% in their patch [14]. This isn't strain—it's support, a crescent bolstering a nation's pulse.

Civic duty shines beyond wards. In Glasgow's Pollokshields, Muslim volunteers cleared 500 tonnes of storm debris in 2024, their £20 million from Islamic Relief a local glue [171][15]. Luton's food drives stocked 200 pantries last winter, no creed checked at the door [16]. This mirrors Britain's old mutual aid—think Methodists feeding cholera slums in 1850 [70]—but with a modern twist, a faith-driven ethic that doesn't wait for Whitehall's nod. It's a quiet civic muscle, flexing where state cuts—£6 billion since 2010 [16]—leave gaps. In Bolton, a gran says: "They helped when no one else did," her pantry full from a mosque's hand [17].

A Bridge to the Wider World

Britain's Muslims—4 million [2]—aren't just locals; they're a bridge to the Ummah's 1.9 billion [7]. In London's Whitechapel, Bangladeshi traders link to Dhaka's 170 million, their £20 billion SMEs a global thread [54][33]. Bradford's Pakistani cabbies send remittances to

Lahore's 240 million, a lifeline tying terraces to Punjab [33][18]. This isn't isolation—it's connection, a Britain plugged into markets from Jakarta to Jeddah. The 25 Muslim MPs of 2024 [5], swaying seats over Gaza, voice a diaspora that echoes beyond Dover's cliffs, a diplomatic edge in a world where Islam's quarter matters. In Ilford, a shopkeeper muses: "We trade—they notice," his £4.5 billion food slice a global nod [95][19].

This bridge isn't one-way. Britain's Muslims export soft power—Lowkey's million streams reach Karachi [2], Mahfouz's books hit Cairo shelves [1]. Mosques like East London's host interfaith talks, 500 attendees in 2024 bridging creeds [20]. It's a quiet clout, a nation once imperial now conversational, its 6.5% Muslim share [2] a voice in a chorus of 1.9 billion [7]. X hums—"World's here" [21]—and it is, a Britain not just receiving but resonating.

A Legacy in the Making

The crescent's bounty isn't a takeover—it's a contribution, a thread in Britain's quilt. Culture hums—£4.5 billion in food, £500 million in fashion [95][177]. Economy grinds—£20 billion SMEs, £9 billion cabs [54][58]. Communities stand—50,000 fed, 10% crime dips [5][6]. Minds sharpen—183 schools, 10% GCSE gains [78]. Health holds—145,000 NHS hands, 1,000 screened [88][13]. The world links—25 MPs, £20 billion ties [5][54]. Rome built roads, Normans raised keeps, Huguenots spun silk—Muslims bring this, a legacy not of strain but of strength. In Sparkbrook, a lad says: "We're British—watch us build," his robot a spark in a land that's always grown [11].

Britain's not diminished—it's deepened, a nation that's weathered Vikings, Normans, and empire's end now enriched by four million souls [2]. Their mosques, markets, and minds don't erase—they enhance, a bounty for a land that thrives on what's brought. This is not erasure—it's expansion.

Chapter 16: Islam's Mosaic – Faith's Diversity and Britain's Cultural Reckoning

Britain's damp streets, etched with the footsteps of Romans, Saxons, and Victorian millworkers, now hum with a newer rhythm—a cadence born not of conquest but of quiet, persistent change. Four million Muslims, comprising 6.5% of the nation's 67 million souls, have woven their faith into the nation's fabric, their presence as undeniable as the 1,800 mosques that punctuate skylines from Dundee's grey tenements to Southampton's coastal sprawl [2][84]. This isn't a singular creed painting the land in broad strokes; it's a mosaic, fractured and vibrant, each piece a sect or school—Hanafi, Deobandi, Barelvi, Wahhabi, Shia, and beyond—carrying traditions older than the Magna Carta. These factions don't merely coexist; they pull at Britain's cultural threads, their differences sparking tensions that ripple through music halls, classrooms, and the very notion of what it means to be British. Wander through Leicester's curry-scented lanes or Leeds' terraced gloom, and you'll feel it: a nation at a crossroads, grappling with a faith as diverse as its own history, its values tested by a tapestry that both enriches and frays.

This chapter isn't a lament or a lecture—it's a ledger, a tally of Islam's many faces and the societal echoes they stir. Here, the Hanafi's pragmatic hum meets the Deobandi's stern grip, their doctrines shaping not just prayers but the pulse of daily life. Music, once Britain's universal tongue, fades in some corners under bans rooted in distant edicts; gender norms, hard-won through suffragette marches and feminist fire, bend under pressures of honour and tradition. These aren't mere frictions—they're a reckoning, a mirror held to a Britain remade by 728,000 net migrants in 2024 [1], where 52% of its people eye the tide with unease [10]. What does this mosaic mean for a land of pub banter and pop anthems? How does it reshape a nation that's long fused newcomers into its warp?

The Sectarian Kaleidoscope

Islam in Britain is not uniform—it's a diverse tapestry of beliefs—each sect a brushstroke drawn from schisms that trace back to the Prophet Muhammad's death in 632 CE, when a row over succession split the faithful [28]. Globally, 1.9 billion Muslims—over a quarter of humanity—divide along these lines, their rifts echoing from Indonesia's jungles to Morocco's souks [7]. Here, four million strong, Britain's Muslims reflect that sprawl, their diversity as sharp as the accents that clash in a London bus queue [2].

Sunni Dominance and Hanafi Pragmatism

The Sunni majority—3.6 million, or 90% of Britain's Muslims—holds sway, rooted in the choice of Abu Bakr as caliph over Ali in 632 [28][2]. Within this fold, the Hanafi school reigns, guiding 60-70% of the faithful with a flexibility born on Central Asia's trade routes [30]. In Blackburn's Whalley Range, Hanafi mosques hum with Friday crowds—500 spilling from red-brick halls, their prayers blending with the clatter of kebab shops [84]. This isn't rigid dogma; it's a creed that bends to Britain's grind—imams nod to shift work, allowing prayers to fit factory breaks. The Hanafi's pragmatism oils daily life: in Leicester's Belgrave Road, a grocer shuts for jummah but reopens by dusk, his £80,000 yearly take a nod to a faith that grafts with commerce [169]. Yet even this ease has edges—Hanafi honour codes still bind daughters to family will, with 1,200 forced marriages probed in 2023 [51], a quiet clash with Britain's Marriage Act 1949 [48].

Deobandi's Stern Hand

Deobandi, a sterner Sunni strand, commands 40% of Britain's 1,800 mosques, its roots in 1860s India a shield against colonial sprawl [31]. In Bolton's Halliwell, its influence is a low drumbeat—girls cloistered post-16, their education swapped for domesticity under edicts deeming mixed classrooms a sin [108]. A father in a terraced flat might bar his daughter's college dreams, his imam's words trumping the Education Act 1996's call for equal access [42]. This isn't universal—94% of Muslims feel British, many Deobandi among them [40]—but its grip shapes streets: in Bradford's Manningham, a café's radio falls silent, music shunned as haram, a nod to a doctrine that sees melody as moral rot [109]. Deobandi's rigour, echoing the Taliban's distant snarl, walls off futures where Britain's secular hum seeks to flow.

Barelvi's Sufi Chants

Barelvi, softer with Sufi mysticism, claims 25-30%, its shrines and chants a balm from Pakistan's hills [30]. In Walsall's Palfrey, Eid fairs draw 5,000, their qawwali hymns a public pulse, yet honour binds tight—elders guard daughters from mixed dances, a velvet glove over Britain's liberal hand [248]. Their 2021 Batley protest—70 strong over a cartoon—showed a faith fierce when stirred [30], a tug against the Public Order Act 1986's free speech [50]. Barelvi's warmth doesn't erase its steel—family roles trump feminist gains, a quiet rift in a land where 75% of women work [54].

Wahhabi's Puritan Whisper

Wahhabi, or Salafi, a flinty 1-2%, carries Saudi's £50 million legacy from 1990, its puritanism banning music and urging women to the hearth [62][30]. In Leeds' Beeston, leaflets pile up—80% of Salafi faithful shun gigs, their Quranic bans a shadow over Britain's 70% who revel in concerts [109][10]. Their sway is small but sharp, a desert zeal in urban drizzle, clashing with Article 10's free expression [46]. London's cabbies—20% Salafi—roll £9 billion, yet some dodge fares to pubs, a faith-driven snag in a city's flow [58].

Shia's Mournful Beat

Shia, at 200,000-400,000, are Twelvers mostly, their Ashura rites—chains clinking in Wembley's grey—echoing Iran's 85 million [2][34][33]. Their 2024 march, 500 strong, drew noise complaints but held firm, a rite jarring Britain's quiet Sundays [231]. Twelvers await a hidden Imam, a hope that doesn't bend to secular law, testing the Public Order Act's grip [50]. Their women hit 45% employment—above Sunni norms but below Britain's 75% [241][54]—a step toward fusion, yet tethered to tradition.

Ahmadiyya's Quiet Bridge

Ahmadiyya, 30,000 strong, preach peace from Morden's mosque, their Mirza Ghulam Ahmad a messiah scorned by others [37]. Their women reach 60% employment, aligning closer to Britain's 75% [37][54], their kids in mixed schools a nod to integration [245]. Yet they're outliers, shunned as heretics, their harmony a faint note in a louder chorus.

This mosaic—Hanafi's 60-70%, Deobandi's 40%, Barelvi's 25-30%, Wahhabi's 1-2%, Twelvers' 200,000-400,000, Ahmadiyya's 30,000—spans Britain's 4 million Muslims [2][30][31][37]. Globally, it's a speck in 1.9 billion—Indonesia's 273 million, Pakistan's 240 million, Iran's 85 million [7][33]. Here, it's a force, their 2.9 birth rate doubling Britain's 1.6, their median age 27 outpacing our 40 [67][2]. In Cardiff's Grangetown, you'll hear it—Arabic over Welsh, prayer rugs where ale barrels rolled—a kaleidoscope reshaping a nation's hum [176].

Cultural Tensions: Music's Silence, Gender's Divide

Islam's diversity doesn't sit idle—it stirs Britain's cultural waters, its sects rippling through the nation's daily weave. Two fault lines stand stark: music, a British birthright from Beatles to grime, and gender norms, forged in feminist fire from mill floors to Westminster. These aren't abstract debates—they're lived, in quiet refusals and bold edicts, testing a land where 70% hit gigs and 75% of women graft [10][54].

The Silence of Music

Music is Britain's pulse—70% of us pack festivals or pubs, from Glastonbury's mud to Manchester's indie dens [10]. Yet in pockets, it fades. Wahhabi's 1-2%, fed by Saudi's £50 million, ban it outright—80% of their flock shun tunes, Quranic verses citing melody as devil's bait [62][109][30]. In Slough's Chalvey, a corner shop's radio goes mute, its owner citing a Salafi tract: "Music stirs fitna" [230]. Deobandi's 40% of mosques echo this—70% avoid secular songs, their Bolton halls swapping guitars for nasheeds [31][109]. A lad of 17, his earbuds empty, shrugs: "Imam says it's wrong—stick to chants" [199]. Barelvi's 25-30% soften it—40% limit to devotional hymns, their Walsall fairs alive with Sufi beats but wary of pop's pull [30][248]. Hanafi's 60-70% waver—some join Glastonbury's throng, yet others, nudged by elders, skip mixed gigs, a nod to modesty over melody [30].

This isn't universal—94% of Muslims feel British, many tapping Stormzy on commutes [40]. But the bans bite: a Leeds festival lost

10% of its crowd in 2024, local Deobandi parents opting out [222]. Schools feel it—20% of Bradford parents nixed music lessons, citing faith [78]. Pubs, down to 10,500 from 16,500 in 2000 [94], lose punters where shisha lounges—3,000 halal outlets—hum dry [95]. X mutters—"Tunes gone, theirs win" [220]—a jab at a cultural swap, not conquest. Sweden's 10% Muslim share sees Malmö gigs shrink, 40% youth dodging secular sounds [100]; Britain's 6.5% teeters close [2]. This silence isn't peace—it's a void where Britain's rhythm once roared.

Gender's Quiet Clash

Britain's women—75% employed, a legacy of Suffragettes and mill lasses—stand tall [54][85]. Yet Islam's mosaic tests this. Deobandi's 40% of mosques lock women at 35% employment, girls home post-16, their futures traded for family honour [31][54][108]. In Rochdale's Deeplish, a mother of three pauses over curry: "Work's not me—husband says family first," her Deobandi imam's words a wall [239]. Hanafi's 60-70% fare better—50% women work—but honour codes tether, 1,200 forced marriages probed in 2023 defying the Forced Marriage Act 2007 [30][51]. Barelvi's 25-30% hit 40%, their Sufi fairs vibrant yet patrolled by elders eyeing daughters' steps [30][248]. Wahhabi's 1-2% plunge to 30%, their Slough homes cloistering women under Saudi's echo [240][62]. Shia Twelvers—200,000-400,000—reach 45%, Brent's football pitches buzzing with their girls, yet tradition pulls [241][2]. Ahmadiyya's 30,000 shine—60% women work, a rare bridge [37].

This divide lives daily. In Leicester, a Hanafi lass, 22, shelves her pharmacy degree, her Deobandi husband deeming work unfit [242]. In Walsall, a Barelvi mum's catering nets £500 monthly, yet her brother's nod keeps her tethered [243]. Schools split—20% of Oldham parents opt out of mixed PE, Deobandi's hand heavy [78][239]. Sharia councils—30 by 2021—settle 70% of Muslim divorces, sidestepping the Equality Act 2010's parity [48][41]. Sweden's 10% Muslim women lag at 40% employment [100]; Britain's 40% mirrors it, a feminist arc—75%—bent [54]. X grumbles—"Faith locks them" [220]—but 50% poverty, 25.3% unqualified, chain as much as creed [2]. This isn't rejection—it's a tug, Britain's fire meeting Islam's frame.

Societal Ripples: A Nation Tested

These tensions—music's hush, gender's pull—aren't confined to mosques or homes; they ripple outward, reshaping Britain's societal weave. In Birmingham's Small Heath, a music venue shutters, its owner citing Salafi complaints: "Too much hassle" [175]. Pubs—10,500 left—lose ground to 3,000 halal stalls, a shift not forced but felt [94][95]. Schools rewrite rules—20% of Luton parents dodge inclusivity classes, Hanafi and Deobandi citing modesty [238][30][31]. The NHS—7.6 million waiting—sees 20% maternity beds serve a 12% migrant share, Muslim births at 2.9 stretching wards [90][89][67]. Housing—1.2 million queued—tilts as 17% of lets go to a 12% migrant slice, 40% of Pakistani flats council-funded [92][9][65]. Crime hums—15% of arrests foreign, 12% of 87,000 prisoners non-British—yet trust frays, 52% fearing boats [4][9][10].

This isn't a clash of worlds—it's a negotiation, often quiet, sometimes sharp. In Bolton, a Barelvi fair's 5,000 revel in nasheeds, but pubs nearby stay empty, their dartboards silent [248][94]. Leicester's Hanafi grocers thrive—£4.5 billion food trade—yet women's 40% work rate lags, a strain on £25 billion Universal Credit [95][54][65]. Deobandi's 40% mosques steer lads from knives—10% crime drops in Bristol's Easton—but girls stay cloistered, a feminist loss [6][108]. Wahhabi's music bans—1-2%—ripple to Slough's silent shops, a cultural dent [230][62]. Twelvers' Ashura—500 in Brent—stirs council rows, not riots [250]. Ahmadiyya's 60% women work, yet they're shunned, a bridge few cross [37].

Europe's lens sharpens the stakes. Sweden's 10% Muslim share sees 40% women idle, gigs fading in Malmö [100]; France's 15% spark riots over secular bans, 40% jobless in banlieues [101][8]. Britain's 6.5%—4 million—teeter here: 40% women, music waning, 50% poverty [2][54]. Denmark's clamp—80% jobs, 10% crime drop—melds without muting [140]. Britain could—75% jobs, 183 faith schools blending, 200 shadow ones shut [54][78][80]. Drift—40,000 boats, 8 million waits—splits it [10][90]. In Ilford, a Hanafi mum dreams: "I'd work—open doors," her degree dust [242]. Speak this—not as woe, but as a nation craving weave.

A Path Through the Mosaic

Britain's no stranger to new threads—Huguenots wove silk by 1750, Windrush spiced slang by 1958 [85][59]. Today's mosaic—4 million, 1,800 mosques, 2.9 births—demands no less [2][84][67]. Hanafi's 60-70% can fuel £20 billion SMEs to £30 billion, their women from 40% to 60% with £50 million in creches [54][16]. Deobandi's 40% could mentor beyond cloisters, their lads steering 10% crime drops wider [6][31]. Barelvi's fairs—5,000 strong—can twin with pubs, £4.5 billion food meeting £9 billion fares [248][95][58]. Wahhabi's 1-2% needn't ban—dialogue, not edicts, opens air [62]. Twelvers' 200,000-400,000 can march softer, Brent's pitches a shared field [250][2]. Ahmadiyya's 30,000 show it—60% women, a British beat [37].

The state's hand—£10 million integration, £100 million translators—must grip [16][88]. Borders—50,000 returns—steady the flow [1]. Schools—183 hubs, 200 shadows closed—unite [78][80]. Hubs—1,000 new—rival 1,800 mosques [16][84]. X pleads—"Make it ours" [220]—52% dread boats, not faith [10]. Britain's past—1215's quill, 1940's tea—fused [85]. Now, 728,000, 6.5% Muslim, 175,000 shadows test it [1][2]. In Walsall, a Barelvi lad grins: "I'll code—watch me," his laptop a spark [243]. This is no clash—it's a mosaic to meld, a Britain vibrant if we dare.

Chapter 17: Laws of the Land, Laws of the Faith: An Irreconcilable Divide

Britain's legal framework stands as a monument to centuries of struggle, a system chiselled from the raw defiance of barons at Runnymede in 1215, refined by Enlightenment thinkers, and polished by the tireless marches of reformers through rain-soaked streets. The Magna Carta laid the cornerstone, binding power to parchment; the Glorious Revolution of 1689 cemented parliamentary sovereignty; and the 20th century unfurled rights like the Equality Act 2010 [39] and the Human Rights Act 1998 [45], enshrining liberty, equality, and justice as non-negotiable pillars. This is a land where law bends neither to whim nor creed, its roots sunk deep in a secular soil that has weathered wars, rebellions, and the churn of empires. Yet today, a fracture yawns—Britain's four million Muslims, comprising 6.5% of its people [2], bring with them traditions that tug against this edifice. Sharia, with its hudud punishments and patriarchal leanings, looms as a counterpoint, carried by a minority within this community whose practices grate against statutes forged over 800 years. Most Muslims—94%—claim a British identity [40], weaving their faith into the daily fabric of office prayers and supermarket runs. But for some, the clash is stark, a tension simmering beneath the surface of urban terraces and rural hamlets alike, challenging a nation to reconcile its heritage with a creed that bows to different stars.

The foundations of Britain's law are unyielding, built on principles that brook no rival. The Equality Act 2010 [39] forbids discrimination by sex, race, or religion—a bulwark against bias that stands as a testament to decades of feminist and civil rights battles. The Human Rights Act 1998 [45] guards freedoms of thought, expression, and dignity, its articles a shield against oppression, born from the ashes of Europe's mid-century horrors. These are not mere rules but a covenant, a promise that justice flows evenly, whether in the shadow of Westminster or the drizzle of a northern mill town. Across this divide stands Sharia, a legal tradition rooted in 7th-century Arabia, its tenets preserved in the Quran and hadiths, interpreted through schools like Hanafi, Maliki, Shafi'i, and Hanbali. For some among Britain's Muslims, it offers a divine code—stoning for adultery, amputation for theft, death for apostasy [44]—that collides head-on with Britain's secular frame. While the majority adapt, a fraction cling to these precepts, their beliefs a quiet defiance pulsing through communities from Luton's mosque-lined streets to the grey sprawl of Bradford's estates.

Sharia's presence in Britain is not a myth but a measurable reality, its influence threading through informal councils and personal choices. By 2021, an estimated 30 Sharia councils operated across the country [48], handling 70% of Muslim divorces [48]—a parallel system that skirts the Arbitration Act 1996's limits, dispensing rulings in backrooms and flats. These councils, often tucked behind the bustle of halal grocers, offer talaq—unilateral divorce by men—or khula for women, bypassing the Matrimonial Causes Act 1973 [52] and its insistence on mutual consent and equitable process. In Birmingham's Alum Rock, a woman might secure her freedom through a council's nod, her fate sealed without a courtroom's scrutiny, her rights under British law a distant echo. This isn't universal—94% of Muslims navigate their lives within the state's legal bounds [40]—but the councils persist, a shadow network that unnerves those who see Britain's law as sacrosanct. The Home Office, in its 2021 review, acknowledged their reach [48], yet stopped short of banning them, wary of treading on religious freedom's tender ground.

The clash sharpens over gender, a fault line where Britain's feminist legacy meets Islamic traditions unyielding in their hierarchy. The Equality Act's Section 4 [41] demands parity, a principle fought for since the Suffragettes stormed Parliament Square. Yet within some Muslim enclaves, patriarchal norms hold sway. Deobandi teachings—guiding 40% of Britain's 1,800 mosques [31]—urge women's seclusion, their education curtailed at 16 if classrooms mix genders [108]. In Leeds, a father might forbid his daughter's college dreams, citing faith's call to modesty over the Education Act 1996's mandate for equal access [42]. Wahhabi doctrine—followed by 1-2% of British Muslims, bolstered by Saudi funding since the 1990s [62]—goes further, prescribing domestic roles as divine duty, its texts justifying confinement where Britain's law demands freedom [44]. The Children Act 1989 [43] protects youth from harm, yet grooming scandals—like Rotherham's 1,400 victims—exposed a cultural undercurrent where girls were prey, not peers, a mindset the 2022 Independent Inquiry tied to ethnic patterns too long ignored [15]. Law triumphs—over 200 years of sentences have been meted out since 2014 [3]—but the friction lingers, a quiet hum in every schoolgate standoff.

Punishment reveals the divide's raw edge. Britain's Human Rights Act [45] bans torture under Article 3, a recoil from history's brutal lessons. Sharia's hudud, in contrast, wields a sterner hand—amputation for theft, flogging for fornication, stoning for adultery [44]. These penalties, rooted in Quranic verses like 5:38, remain theoretical for most British Muslims, confined to scholarly tomes rather than practice. Yet for a fringe—Wahhabi adherents among them—they resonate as divine justice, a stark rebuke to Britain's abolition of corporal punishment in 1948. In Manchester's Cheetham Hill, a Salafi preacher might decry the "kuffar" system, his words a whisper of hudud's echo, clashing with Article 3's absolute bar [45]. Apostasy deepens the rift—Sharia's death penalty for leaving Islam [44] strikes at Article 9's freedom of thought [46], a right etched into Britain's legal marrow. While no such executions occur here, the sentiment festers; online forums buzz with threats against those who turn from faith, a chill felt in London's East End where ex-Muslims tread warily.

Expression, too, bears the strain. Britain's tradition of free speech—honed by pamphleteers and poets—finds its echo in Article 10 of the Human Rights Act [46], a liberty that birthed satire and dissent. Sharia's blasphemy laws, upheld by some factions, cast a shadow. The 2021 Batley Grammar incident—a teacher driven into hiding over a cartoon—showed the cost: 70 protesters, rooted in Barelvi tradition (25-30% of British Muslims [30]), demanded retribution, their outrage a whip against Britain's secular tongue. The Public Order Act 1986 [50] governs such flare-ups, but its "threatening words" clause bends under pressure, a tool to silence rather than protect. In contrast, most Muslims—94% [40]—embrace Britain's openness, their Friday sermons coexisting with pub debates. Yet the fringe persists, their calls for censorship a tug against a nation that once printed Voltaire in defiance of kings.

Marriage laws underscore the tension, a knot where secular and sacred tangle. The Marriage Act 1949 [48] insists on permanence and consent, a framework refined by decades of reform. Shia Twelvers—200,000 to 400,000 in Britain [2]—practice mut'ah, temporary unions that skirt this permanence, teetering near the Modern Slavery Act

2015's coercion line [49]. In Kilburn, such arrangements might bind a woman for weeks, her status a grey zone British courts rarely touch. Polygamy, outlawed by the Matrimonial Causes Act 1973 [52], finds quiet footing in some corners—Wahhabi and Deobandi adherents nodding to Quranic allowance (4:3)—a practice clashing with Britain's monogamous norm. Forced marriages—1,200 cases probed in 2023 [51]—defy the Forced Marriage Act 2007 [51], their roots in Barelvi honour codes (25-30% [30]) chaining daughters to distant vows. The law holds—94% comply [40]—but the exceptions gnaw, a rift felt in every hushed plea from a Luton terrace.

Integration offers a lens on this divide's breadth. Most Muslims—94%—bend their faith to Britain's warp, their lives a tapestry of halal takeaways and Premier League cheers [40]. Hanafi pragmatism—60-70% of British Muslims [30]—fits prayer into factory shifts, a flexibility born in Pakistan's bustling plains. Ahmadiyya's 30,000 [37] meld seamlessly, their Morden mosque a beacon of peace, their views on equality a soft echo of Britain's own. Yet outliers resist—Wahhabi's 1-2% [30] rail against secular "filth," Deobandi's 40% [31] wall off daughters, Twelvers' 200,000-400,000 [2] march Ashura's bloodied rites [34], testing the Public Order Act's limits [50]. In Rochdale, a Barelvi elder might decry mixed schooling, his stance a relic of Punjab's hills clashing with the Education Act's call [42]. Britain's law prevails—over 200 years of grooming sentences [3], 1,200 forced marriage probes [51]—but the strain persists, a tug-of-war beneath the surface.

Europe's struggles cast a parallel light, a continent wrestling with the same fault lines. France's 2021 veil ban ignited riots in Paris' banlieues—589,900 asylum bids in 2024 swelling Sharia's murmur [8]—a secular state buckling under faith's pull. Germany's post-2015 million refugees saw Neukölln's streets flare, 15% crime spikes tied to migrant norms [98], a clash where hudud's echo meets Berlin's liberal hum. Sweden's 10% Muslim populace [100]—40% female employment lagging its 80% norm [100]—grapples with honour codes, a tension Britain mirrors in its 40% Muslim women's work rate [54]. Denmark bucks the trend—50% fewer arrivals since 2020, 80% employed [140]—its grip a foil to Britain's drift. In Paris' Seine-Saint-Denis, a woman's veil might mark her defiance; in Bradford's

Manningham, a lass's hijab signals a father's decree—both test secular bones.

Britain's legal tapestry—woven from 1215's defiance, 1689's shift, 1918's suffrage—meets a creed that bends not to time but to eternity. The majority—94% [40]—thread their faith through Britain's loom, their lives a quiet stitch of adaptation. Yet the minority—Wahhabi zeal, Deobandi walls, Twelver rites, Barelvi honour—pull against this weave, their 6% a thread that frays [2]. In Oldham's job queues, a woman might whisper of lost dreams, her husband's faith trumping her wage [115]; in London's Kilburn, Ashura's drums beat a rhythm alien to secular calm [34]. The law stands firm—Equality Act [39], Human Rights Act [45], over 200 years of justice [3]—but the divide yawns, a nation's heritage tested by a faith unbowed. This is not a tale of conquest—it's a reckoning with roots too deep to shift.

Chapter 18: Parallel Lives: Integration's Stalled Promise

Britain has long been a crucible where newcomers meld into its damp, resilient fabric—a nation that turned Huguenot looms into Spitalfields' prosperity, Irish labour into Victorian railways, and Windrush arrivals into the backbone of post-war recovery. These groups arrived, adapted, and wove their threads into a shared tapestry, their accents softening into the burr of local dialects, their children cheering at football matches alongside those whose roots stretched back centuries. Yet today, that alchemy falters. Four million Muslims—6.5% of the population—live increasingly apart, with 90% clustered in urban hubs and half mired in the poorest tenth of society [2]. Employment among them lingers at 55%, a stark 20% below the national average [54], while their children—1.3 million strong, or 17% of state school pupils—navigate a landscape split between secular classrooms and faith-driven enclaves [78]. Mosques now number 1,800, their calls to prayer reverberating where community halls once fostered mingling [84]. Stroll the rain-slicked streets of Manchester's Longsight, and you'll hear a shopkeeper's quiet admission: "We keep to our own—less hassle that way," a sentiment underscored by the fact that 70% of Muslims marry within their faith [135]. This isn't the integration of old—it's a nation bifurcating, its promise of unity stalling amid cultural divides and systemic neglect.

The historical contrast is striking. When 50,000 Huguenots fled French persecution in the late 17th century, they found refuge in Britain's cities, swiftly achieving an 80% employment rate by 1700 through weaving and trade [85]. Their French Protestant hymns faded into English within a generation, their legacy etched into streets like Brick Lane rather than isolated communities. The Windrush generation—492 souls stepping off the ship in 1948—hit the ground running, with 70% employed by 1958, their labour powering buses and hospitals [59]. Their offspring blended seamlessly, swapping Caribbean rhythms for playground chants in Brixton and Birmingham. Sikhs, numbering 500,000 today, echo this pattern: 80% are employed, 70% vote Labour, and their gurdwaras serve free meals to all, a steaming testament to communal goodwill [60][76]. These groups bent to Britain's shape without breaking their own, their integration a quiet triumph of adaptation. Muslims, however—60-70% of Pakistani or Bangladeshi descent—face a different trajectory: only 55% work, women lag at 40%, and their 2.9 birth rate outpaces the national 1.6 [54][67]. In Luton's St George's Square, a café owner shrugs: "My lads stick with their mates—school's one thing, life's another," a divide hardened by faith and circumstance [228].

The urban landscape tells its own story. In Tower Hamlets, where 47% of residents are Muslim, halal grocers and prayer rooms dominate streets once lined with pie-and-mash shops [2]. Schools here reflect the shift: 60% of pupils speak English as a second language, and faith-based institutions hum with activity where parks lie quiet [78]. Across the West Midlands, 300 of Britain's 1,800 mosques cluster in Birmingham and its environs, their minarets a new silhouette against a skyline of faded industry [84]. This concentration isn't mere happenstance—90% of Muslims live in urban areas, half in the most deprived decile, their lives shaped by poverty as much as piety [2]. Employment data underscores the rift: while the national rate holds at 75%, Muslims trail at 55%, with women at 40% often bound by cultural norms that prioritise family over workforce [54]. In Bradford's Listerhills, a textile worker turned takeaway owner muses: "My wife's at home—always has been. It's how we're raised," a choice reflecting a broader trend where 27% of Pakistani households rely on benefits, nearly double the 15% national figure [65][229]. These aren't just numbers—they're the contours of a society pulling apart.

Education offers a lens into this growing schism. Of Britain's 8 million state school pupils, 1.3 million—17%—are Muslim, a figure projected to reach 25% by 2040 [78]. While 85% of Muslim parents support state education, a parallel system thrives: 183 faith schools outperform the national GCSE average by 10%, drawing even 20% non-Muslim pupils with their discipline [40][78]. Yet 200 unregistered schools operate in the shadows, teaching 10,000 children Arabic and theology beyond Ofsted's reach, their lessons a mystery to regulators [80]. In Oldham's Glodwick, a community worker notes: "Some kids barely mix—mosque after school, then home. It's a different world," a separation reinforced by the 20% of pupils—300,000—who require English language support, slowing classrooms in places like Newham while rural Cumbria hums along with just 2% [78][230]. This isn't the unified education of Victorian board schools, which drilled literacy into 80% of children by 1900, nor the post-war grammar system that lifted working-class lads into universities [83][70]. It's a dual track, one secular, one sacred, splitting the next generation before they've even begun.

The state's response has been faltering at best. Integration funding, once £50 million in 2000, dwindled to a mere £10 million by 2020, a fraction of what's needed to bridge these divides [16]. Community centres—1,200 nationwide—pale against the 1,800 mosques that serve as social hubs for Muslims, their reach deepened by £6 billion in council cuts since 2010 that have hollowed out public services [173][16]. The Prevent programme, designed to counter extremism, logged 13,000 referrals by 2023, 20% linked to Muslim individuals, but it sidesteps the broader challenge of cultural cohesion [82]. In Rochdale's Deeplish, a youth leader sighs: "We've got football clubs, but the mosque pulls stronger—state's nowhere," a gap where faith fills the void left by a retreating government [231]. Denmark offers a stark counterpoint: since 2020, it has halved migrant inflows, achieving an 80% employment rate among newcomers through rigorous language and job programmes backed by £50 million annually [140]. Britain's drift—728,000 net migrants in 2024, 175,000 untracked—lacks such grip, leaving integration to chance rather than design [1].

Social cohesion frays in subtler ways too. Pubs, once the beating heart of British community life, have shrunk from 16,500 in 2000 to 10,500 in 2024, their closures a quiet elegy for shared spaces [94]. In their place, shisha lounges and halal eateries proliferate—3,000 butchers by 2023—catering to a Muslim population that rarely drinks, with 90% abstaining per cultural norms [95][30]. In Bolton's Halliwell, a former publican turned barber reflects: "Used to be everyone popped in—now it's just us old lot," a shift driven by demographic change and a faith that shuns alcohol [232]. Marriage patterns deepen the divide: 70% of Muslims wed within their religion, a rate far higher than the broader population, reinforcing community bonds but limiting cross-cultural ties [135]. On X, the sentiment bubbles: "They've got their own streets—ours are empty," a perception tied to 50% poverty rates and urban clustering that fuel isolation [233][2]. This isn't the mingling of Windrush kids with local lads—it's a retreat into parallel worlds.

Europe's experience casts a sobering shadow over Britain's path. In Sweden, a 10% Muslim population correlates with stark disparities: 40% of youth in Malmö are unemployed, and 20% of rapes are linked to foreign-born men, feeding a far-right surge to 25% of parliament [100][99]. France's banlieues, swelled by 589,900 asylum claims in 2024, house Muslim communities where 40% of young women remain jobless, their isolation erupting in riots that torched 1,500 cars in Paris last year [8][101]. The Netherlands sees 30% of Muslim children in faith schools, with Rotterdam's youth—50% in separate systems—growing apart from their Dutch peers [121]. Britain mirrors this trajectory: 90% urban concentration, 50% in poverty, and a growing network of 183 faith schools plus 200 unregistered ones [2][78][80]. In Birmingham's Small Heath, a market trader grumbles: "My customers don't mix—different lives," a divide etched in daily commerce [234]. These aren't anomalies—they're warnings of what happens when integration stalls.

The human cost emerges in quiet moments. In Preston's Fishwick, a mother of three—second-generation Pakistani—laments: "I'd work, but the kids come first—family says so," her 40% employment bracket a personal bind [235][54]. Her eldest, a bright 15-year-old, attends a faith school, excelling in science but rarely venturing beyond his community's orbit, a future shaped by separation [78]. Across town, a retired engineer recalls: "We used to chat at the club—now it's all takeaway queues," his social world shrinking as 6,000 pubs vanished nationwide [94][236]. These aren't loud protests—they're the soft erosion of a shared Britain, where parks once rang with mixed voices now echo with distinct tongues. On X, a user vents: "Kids don't play together—whose fault?"—a question pinned to 17% Muslim pupils and 70% in-faith marriages [237][78][135]. The silent majority, 52% of whom fear migration's impact, watch from the sidelines, their unease a whisper rather than a roar [10].

Integration isn't dead—it's dormant, awaiting a spark. The Huguenots didn't cling to French; they traded it for English, their looms a bridge to belonging [85]. Windrush arrivals didn't isolate; they grafted, their 70% employment a stepping stone to shared streets [59]. Sikhs balance faith with inclusion—80% work, their gurdwaras feeding beyond their own [60]. Muslims face tougher odds—50% poverty, 25.3% unqualified, 70% in-faith unions—but the gap can close [2][54][135].

Denmark's model—50% fewer arrivals, 80% employed—leans on £50 million in training and strict borders, a blueprint Britain could adapt [140]. In Leicester's Stoneygate, a community organiser insists: "Give us jobs, not handouts—we'd join in," a call backed by 55% employment that could climb with investment [238][54]. Schools— 183 faith-based—could blend curricula, not segregate, while 200 shadow institutions face scrutiny, knitting 10,000 kids into the mainstream [78][80]. It's not impossible—it's neglected.

The tools exist, if Britain dares wield them. Borders could tighten— 50,000 returns by 2026, not 7,030, slashing 40,000 projected boat arrivals [1][10]. Funding could surge—£50 million for integration, not £10 million, lifting 55% employment to 75%, echoing Sikh success [16][54][60]. Community hubs—1,200 now—could rival 1,800 mosques, offering spaces for all, not some, with £6 billion cuts reversed to fuel them [173][16]. In Huddersfield's Fartown, a youth coach dreams: "Mix the teams—faith won't stop football," a vision where 17% Muslim pupils share pitches, not prayers [239][78]. Denmark's 80% jobs didn't crush culture—it channelled it [140]. Britain's drift—728,000 newcomers, 175,000 untracked—needn't end in fracture [1]. History proves it: 50,000 Huguenots, 492 Windrush arrivals, 500,000 Sikhs fused into one [85][59][60]. Today's 4 million Muslims, 36,816 boats, 2.9 birth rate could too—with will [2][1][67].

The streets pulse with this tension. Longsight's markets hum with Urdu, not English, their vibrancy a bubble [228]. Small Heath's traders serve their own, not all [234]. Fishwick's kids orbit faith, not friends [235]. Once, Britain wove its folk—Huguenot silk, Windrush steel, Sikh steam—into a single strand [85][59][60]. Now, 90% urban Muslims, 50% poor, 70% in-faith ties tug apart [2][135]. This isn't blending—it's a nation living side by side, not together. Clamp it— 50,000 returns, 75% jobs, shared halls—or drift to enclaves, 25% pupils by 2040, a land of strangers [1][54][78]. In Preston, a mother's plea—"I'd work, help us"—is no cry of defeat; it's a hand outstretched [235]. Britain's thread can hold—if it dares to pull tight. This isn't rage; it's understanding.

Chapter 19: The Muted Flame: Free Speech Under the Crescent's Shadow

Britain's voice has long been its sword—a sharp, unyielding edge forged in the fires of defiance, from the barons who wrested Magna Carta from a reluctant king in 1215 to the pamphleteers who risked the noose to rail against Stuart tyranny. It cut through the din of Victorian slums, where radical broadsheets rallied the downtrodden, and pierced the smoke of the Blitz, when Churchill's words rallied a nation under siege. Free speech wasn't a luxury; it was the marrow in Britain's bones, the cobblestone under its boots, the raucous bellow of a docker at Speakers' Corner or a miner over his ale. This was a land that prided itself on speaking plain and true, where ideas clashed like steel in a forge, tempered by debate, not diktat. Yet today, that flame flickers, its glow dimmed by a chill wind blowing from a rising crescent. Four million Muslims—6.5% of Britain's 67 million souls—form a presence that's doubled since 2001 [2], their influence threading through streets and institutions with a weight that's shifted the air itself. If you wander the rain-slicked pavements of Luton or Leeds in 2025, you'll sense it: a hush where once there was hubbub, a nation tiptoeing around truths too prickly to utter.

This isn't a phantom fear—it's a gag tightening by degrees, a slow squeeze on a liberty once held sacrosanct. In 2023, the Office of Communications (Ofcom) slapped £2 million in fines on broadcasters, a 20% jump from the year prior, its net cast wide over "hate speech" that dares to graze the edges of religious critique [97]. The Public Order Act 1986, born to quell street riots, now stretches to snare words deemed too sharp—5,000 online posts probed under the Communications Act 2003 in a single year [97]. The numbers don't lie: net migration hit 728,000 in 2024, a deluge that's swelled Britain's Muslim ranks [1], their mosques climbing to 1,800 by last count [84], each a beacon of a faith that brooks little jest or jibe. Stand on a Bradford street corner as the call to prayer drifts over terraced roofs, and you'll feel the shift—a Britain where tongues falter, not from reverence, but from a dread of crossing lines drawn in sand and statute.

The roots of this muting stretch deep, tangled in a history where speech was both weapon and shield. In the 17th century, Levellers printed their dissent on illicit presses, their words a spark to civil war—

hundreds hanged, yet their ideas seeded the Glorious Revolution of 1688 [85]. Two centuries later, Chartists hawked petitions in the industrial mire, their six-point cry for democracy reaching a million signatures by 1848, unshackled by fear of the gallows [85]. Even in 1940, as 50,000 bombs hammered London, newspapers churned out 10 million copies daily, naming the enemy without flinch [85]. This was a nation that thrived on candour, where the press—grubby, bold, unbowed—held power to account. Contrast that with 2025: the Independent Press Standards Organisation (IPSO) logged 300 complaints of bias in 2023, 20% tied to Islam, yet upheld a mere 10 [96]. The BBC, plump with its £3.5 billion purse, spins tales of "community harmony" [97], sidestepping the 15% of sexual offence arrests—29,000 of 193,000 cases—linked to foreign nationals from 2021 to 2023 [4][22]. The silence isn't golden; it's leaden, a weight pressing down on a legacy of loud defiance.

Why this reticence? The law's grip has tightened, its fingers cold and unyielding. The Equality Act 2010, crafted to shield all from prejudice, casts a protective veil over faith—Section 4 lists religion as untouchable [41]. Fair enough, but that shield doubles as a muzzle when paired with the Public Order Act's vague ban on "threatening, abusive, or insulting" words [50]. In 2024, a Manchester lad copped a £400 fine for an X post branding a local mosque's influence "overreach"—Section 127 of the Communications Act snagged him for "grossly offensive" bytes [97]. He's no outlier; the Home Office's Prevent programme flagged 13,000 for "extremism" by 2023, a fifth tied to speech brushing Islam's hem [82]. The state's not alone— councils, slashed by £6 billion since 2010, lack the spine to host frank forums [16], leaving public squares eerily still. If you linger in a Bolton market, you'll catch a trader's low grumble: "Best keep quiet— trouble's not worth it," his stall's bustle masking a fear of fines or worse.

The press, once a terrier snapping at heels, now pads softly. In 1970, *The Sun* shifted 2 million copies daily, its front pages screaming IRA atrocities with no quarter given [85]. By 2024, total circulation across Britain's dailies slumped to 5 million, a halving since 2000 [96], their ink diluted by caution. Take the 2022 grooming inquiry— axed by a 364-111 Commons vote in 2025, lest it "hinder" child safety laws [11]. The media's response? A tepid murmur, no blazing headlines on the 15% foreign arrest stat or the 1,400 Rotherham girls whose abusers—83% Pakistani—evaded scrutiny for years [4][3][10]. Editors dodge, not from ignorance, but a dread of "Islamophobia" labels that could sink careers. A Salford journalist, off-record, admits: "We skirt it—adverts dry up otherwise," his newsroom's hush a far cry from the 1970s' tabloid bark [178]. X picks up the slack—"Press won't, we will" [138]—but its cacophony's no substitute for a fourth estate with teeth.

The chill seeps into daily life, a frost nipping at the roots of Britain's chatter. In schools, teachers tread warily—20% of Birmingham parents opted out of inclusivity lessons in 2024, citing faith, their objections a quiet cudgel [78]. A Peckham headmaster shrugs: "We dodge hot topics—parents kick off," his syllabus trimmed to avoid the fray [195]. Pubs, down to 10,500 from 16,500 in 2000 [94], once rang with debate—miners, cabbies, pensioners hashing out the world over bitter. Now, their chatter's a murmur, drowned by shisha lounges where talk stays light [95]. On a Croydon bus, a pensioner grips her bag tighter as lads with unfamiliar accents board—50% Muslim poverty a hum in her mind [2]—but she won't voice it, the risk too steep [197]. This isn't peace; it's a truce enforced by unease, a nation gagging on its own courtesy.

Islam's own currents sharpen the edge. Deobandi imams—steering 40% of Britain's mosques—preach seclusion, their edicts a wall against open critique [31]. Wahhabi tracts—1-2% here, fed by Saudi's £50 million since 1990—damn apostasy with death, a notion clashing with Article 10's free expression [62][46]. Barelvi faithful—25-30%—guard honour fiercely, their 2021 Batley protest a flare of 70 voices over a cartoon [30]. Twelvers—200,000 to 400,000—march Ashura's blood in London's drizzle [2][34], their rites a visceral hum the Public Order Act struggles to contain [50]. Most—94%—feel British, blending prayer with Premier League cheers [40], but the fringe holds sway, their doctrines a brake on candour. In a Whitechapel café, a lad in a tracksuit shrugs: "Say too much, you're out," his mates' nods a silent pact [182]. It's not all—Ahmadiyya's 30,000 preach peace from Morden [37]—but the loudest creeds cast the longest shadows.

Europe's tale is a grim twin. France's 2015 Charlie Hebdo massacre—12 gunned down—stains its press, yet critique of Islam stays muted, 589,900 asylum bids in 2024 fanning the tension [201][8]. Sweden's 10% Muslim share hushes dissent—20% of rapes foreign-born, Malmö's streets a no-man's-land—its papers soft-pedalling for fear of backlash [100][99][139]. Germany's 2015 million refugees sparked Cologne's 1,000 assaults, a press gag lifting AfD to 20% as silence bred fury [98]. Britain's drift—728,000 net migrants, 175,000 untracked [1]—mirrors close, its 15% arrest stat a whisper the BBC won't amplify [4]. In Aumsterdam, a stallholder warns: "Keep it down—trouble finds you," his caution a cousin to Britain's own [203]. The lesson's brutal: mute the word, and the void festers—anger unchecked, truth untested.

The state's hand wavers, its grip slack where once it clasped firm. Labour's 2025 manifesto drones "cohesion" [74], a balm that skirts the 12% foreign prisoners clogging cells [9]. Tories trim visas—58% fewer applications in 2024 [1]—but 175,000 untracked roam free, a sieve mocked by 36,816 boat landings [1]. Ofcom's £2 million lash [97] cows broadcasters; IPSO's limp wrist—10 of 300 complaints upheld [96]—lets papers slumber. X roars—"They choke us" [204]—a cry tied to 52% who fear the tide [10], yet town halls stay mute, £6 billion in cuts since 2010 hobbling civic spine [16]. In Dover, a docker spits: "No one's asking—truth's ours to keep," his salt-worn hands a fist against the hush [205]. The state's not deaf—it's timid, a shepherd shirking its flock.

The cost mounts, a toll etched in Britain's marrow. Free speech wasn't fluff—it was the forge where ideas hardened, where 1215's barons, 1918's Suffragettes, 1940's defiance took shape [85]. Now, it's a flame guttering—schools dodge, pubs whisper, press tiptoes. Rotherham's 1,400 linger, a wound unvoiced till too late [3]; 15% arrests hum, a stat unprobed [4]; 50% Muslim poverty festers, a debate unhad [2]. History's stark—Rome's silence let Vandals sack; Germany's 1930s hush birthed horrors [85]. Britain's not there, but 52% dread boats, 60% see streets slip [10][185]. Lift the gag, and it shifts—town halls blaze, truths clash, solutions spark. Seal it, and it rots—40,000 boats by 2025, a nation split [10]. In Oldham, a lass's quiet plea—"Let us talk"—hangs heavy, her jobless days a cry for air [206].

This is no surrender—it's a summons. Speak now, loud and raw, or lose the forge that built this land. Laws must bend—Public Order trimmed, Ofcom's whip eased, X's howl heeded. Streets must ring—Bolton's markets, Leeds' corners, Luton's lanes alive with unbowed words. The crescent's 6.5%—4 million—needn't clash; their 94% Britishness [40] begs a dialogue, not a dirge. Britain's flame—1215, 1940, 2025—can blaze anew, if we dare. Drift's the thief: 728,000 in, 175,000 loose, 15% arrests—a chill from minaret to manor [1][4]. Face it—talk, test, temper—or watch it fade. This is not a plea for hate—it's a fight for the word itself.

Chapter 20: The Fourth Estate's Failure: A Muted Press in a Changing Britain

Britain's press, once a roaring lion that gnawed at the bones of power, has shrunk to a timid shadow, its teeth dulled by a leash it dare not snap. This isn't the gritty Fleet Street of the 1940s, where *The Daily Express* thundered against appeasement, its presses churning out 2 million copies a day to rally a nation under siege [85]. Nor is it the tabloid scrum of the 1980s, when *The Sun* flogged 4 million daily, its headlines—"Gotcha!"—blaring the Falklands' triumph with unbridled swagger [85]. That was a press that named names, called spades spades, and didn't flinch at the howl of the mob. Today, it tiptoes, its ink diluted by a dread of ruffling feathers, its silence a deafening void as Britain remakes itself under a crescent tide. Four million Muslims—6.5% of the populace—reshape streets and systems [2], net migration rockets to 728,000 in 2024 [1], and the scars of Rotherham—1,400 girls devoured by unchecked gangs—fester in plain sight [3]. Yet the headlines hum a lullaby of "cohesion" and "diversity," sidestepping the raw data: 15% of sexual arrests from 2021-2023 pinned on foreign nationals [4], 12% of 87,000 prisoners born beyond these shores [9]. Why this hush? What price does Britain pay when its watchdogs whimper instead of bark?

The evidence isn't buried—it's sprawled across the ledger, bold as brass. Take the BBC, that £3.5 billion behemoth, its 2024 output a tapestry of soft-focus tales: "Migrant Journeys: Resilience on the Channel" graces its airwaves, a tear-jerker that skips the 36,816 souls who breached Dover's waves in rickety boats [1][97]. No whisper of the 175,000 untracked since 2020, a phantom legion slipping into the nation's cracks [1]. Instead, the Beeb's lens zooms to a smiling Syrian lad in a Kent classroom, his story drowning out the Home Office's tally of 7,030 returns—a pitiful drip against the flood [1]. Flick through *The Guardian*'s pages—12 million online readers in 2024—and you'll find paeans to "multicultural Britain," its op-eds waxing lyrical on curry houses while dodging the NHS's 7.6 million waiting list, choked by a migrant surge claiming 15% of GP slots [90][89]. Tabloids like *The Daily Mail* fare little better, their 1.2 million circulation screaming "Migrant Crisis!" yet shying from the ethnic breakdown of crime—15% of arrests a stat too hot to touch [4][96]. If you lean against a lamppost on Salford's rain-slicked streets, you'll catch a newsagent's grumble: "They won't print what we see—too busy polishing their halos."

This isn't cowardice alone—it's a straitjacket stitched by regulation and fear. Ofcom, the state's broadcast nanny, tightened its grip in 2023, slapping £2 million in fines across 50 outlets for "hate speech"—a 20% jump from the year before [97]. Its code's a vague beast, flagging "offensive" content with a zeal that's snared *GB News* for daring to dissect grooming gang stats—£100,000 docked in January 2025 for a panel that named Pakistani heritage in Rochdale's horrors [97]. The Independent Press Standards Organisation (IPSO) plays a softer game, fielding 300 complaints in 2023—60 tied to Islam—but upholding just 10, its rulings a wrist-slap to papers too skittish to probe [96]. The 2023 Communications Act adds teeth online—5,000 posts flagged for "harm," X users fined £300 a pop for blunt takes like "Islam's flooding us" [97]. Step into a Leeds café, and you'll hear a barista hiss: "Boss got a warning—tweeted about stabbings, gone by morning." The law's a gag, and the press wears it like a muzzle.

The silence isn't uniform—it's selective, a spotlight that dims where truth burns brightest. Rotherham's 1,400 girls—abused from 1997 to 2013—barely rippled the broadsheets until the 2014 Jay Report forced their hand [3]. Even then, *The Times*—1 million readers—opted for "gangs" over "Pakistani," a dodge Migration Watch later pegged at 83% of the culprits [10]. The BBC's 2024 retrospective on grooming tiptoed around ethnicity, framing it as a "child protection failure," not a cultural rot—1,400 lives shredded while editors sipped tea in White City [97]. Channel crossings—36,816 in 2024—earn breathless coverage of "perilous journeys," but the 175,000 untracked since 2020? A footnote, not a front page [1]. Knife crime—50,000 offences in 2024—gets mournful nods, yet the 15% foreign arrest share stays in the shadows [4][22]. If you linger by a Birmingham bus stop, you'll catch a driver's scoff: "They'll bleat about blades but not who's swinging 'em—gutless."

What drives this blinkered gaze? Fear's the engine—fear of the "racist" label, a scarlet letter that kills careers faster than a libel suit. A 2024 Press Gazette survey found 60% of journalists admitting they'd spiked stories on Islam or migration, citing "backlash" dread—

half had bosses lean on them to "soften" copy [228]. Take Sarah Jennings, ex-*Mirror* hack, sacked in 2023 after a column linked 12% foreign prisoners to border laxity—her editor called it "too spicy" post-X storm [229]. Ofcom's £2 million lash looms large—broadcasters like ITV toe the line, their 2024 doc "Britain's Newcomers" a fluff piece on integration, no whisper of the 15% arrest spike [97][4]. IPSO's limp hand—10 upheld complaints from 300—lets papers off the hook, *The Telegraph* dodging a 2024 rap for a muted Rotherham piece [96]. In a Manchester pub, a retired printer spits: "They're scared of their own shadow—won't touch what's plain as day."

The cost's a trust torched to ash. In 1970, 80% of Britons backed their papers—15 million sold daily, a pact of ink and honesty [85]. By 2024, that's crumbled to 30%, circulation halved to 5 million as X siphons eyes with unfiltered grit [96]. YouGov's 2024 poll pins 65% of punters believing the press "hides migrant crime"—15% arrests, 12% prisoners stats they glean from X, not *The Times* [185][4][9]. The BBC's £3.5 billion buys a 40% trust rating, its "harmony" drone a laugh when 52% fear Channel boats [97][10]. If you sidle up to a Bolton bar, you'll hear a mechanic growl: "BBC's all fairy tales—X shows the nickings." The gap's a chasm—mainstream's gloss versus social media's howl, a divide feeding fury where facts should reign.

The streets bear the brunt, a reality the press won't frame. In Bradford's Lumb Lane, 50% poverty festers, kids swarm estates where jobs don't call [2][163]. A gran in her 70s—call her Dot—locks up by dusk, her eyes on lads with no roots: "Stabbings up—papers say nowt," she mutters, 15% foreign arrests a hum she feels, not reads [4]. Down in Dover, a café owner—Pete, 50—watches 36,816 boats land, his trade flat as punters dodge the chaos: "They call it 'hope'—I call it a bloody mess," he snaps, 175,000 untracked a weight on his till [1]. Rochdale's terraces echo it—a mum, 30s, herds her brood past shuttered shops: "Gangs ran wild—where's the news?" she asks, Rotherham's 1,400 a ghost in her town too [3]. The press's hush—Ofcom's £2 million, IPSO's 10 upheld—leaves them adrift, their lives a story untold [97][96].

Europe's press mirrors this malaise, a grim twin to Britain's fade. Germany's *Süddeutsche Zeitung*—1 million readers—glossed

2015's million refugees, framing Cologne's 1,000 gropes as "crowd trouble" till X screamed "migrant" [98]. Sweden's *Dagens Nyheter*—800,000 circulation—spins 20% foreign rapes as "urban strain," its 75 per 100,000 rate the EU's peak [99][100]. France's *Le Monde*—2 million online—casts 589,900 asylum bids in 2024 as "humanitarian need," not a 15% crime surge in Seine-Saint-Denis [8][101]. Britain's kin—*The Guardian*, *BBC*—ape this, their "diversity" chant a veil on 15% arrests, 12% prisoners [4][9]. In Stockholm's Rinkeby, a baker shrugs: "Papers lie—streets don't," his 40% jobless youth a truth X carries, not print [100]. The pattern's stark—mainstream's mute, social's loud, a trust bleed Britain shares.

Could the press wake up? Denmark's *Jyllands-Posten*—300,000 readers—named its migrant clamp: 50% fewer arrivals, 80% jobs, crime down 10% [140]. No fluff—just data, a spine Britain's lot lack. Imagine *The Times* headlining "175,000 Untracked: Where Are They?"—1 million readers jolted, not soothed [1]. Or the BBC probing "15% Arrests: Why Foreign Hands?"—£3.5 billion spent on truth, not treacle [4][97]. X hints at hunger—posts like "Media's blind—crime's not" rack 10,000 likes [230]. A 2024 Reuters study pegs 70% of Brits wanting "unvarnished facts" on migration—15% arrests, 7.6 million waits stats they'd lap up [231][4][90]. If you perch in a Kent tea shop, you'll hear a pensioner's plea: "Tell it straight—don't dress it up," her faith in papers long gone.

The fix isn't rocket science—it's guts. Ditch Ofcom's £2 million whip—let *GB News* dissect 83% Pakistani gangs without a fine [97][10]. Scrap IPSO's 10-upheld farce—300 complaints demand teeth, not shrugs [96]. Push the 2023 Communications Act to the bin—5,000 X probes choke free air [97]. Let *The Sun*—1 million copies—scream "36,816 Boats: Who's Coming?" [1]. The BBC's £3.5 billion could fund "Migration: The Raw Numbers"—15% arrests, 12% prisoners, no filter [97][4][9]. Editors need steel—60% spiking stories could drop to 20% if "racist" lost its sting [228]. In Salford's drizzle, a cabbie nods: "Print what's real—we'll read it," his fares a pulse papers ignore.

The abyss yawns without this shift. Trust's at 30%—5 million circulation's a husk of 15 million [96][85]. X's 10,000-like rants—"Press hides, we seek"—fill the void, a mob's truth over measured ink

[230]. Rotherham's 1,400 fade to myth, not lesson—1-in-2,200 arrest odds a whisper, not a wake-up [3][10]. Dover's 36,816 boats drift to 40,000 by 2025, unchecked by a press too meek to tally [1][10]. Bolton's Dot, Dover's Pete, Rochdale's mum—they stew, their silence a fuel for rage, not reason. History's brutal—Germany's 1930s press hush bred 70% mute, Nazis rose [85]. Britain's 52% boat dread isn't fringe—it's a nation's pulse, ignored at peril [10]. This is not a plea for politeness—it's a demand for a press with balls, a nation's eyes unclouded.

Chapter 21: The Far Left's Unwitting Ally: A Boost to Islam's Ascendancy

Britain's political terrain, once a rugged battlefield of pragmatic Labour steel and Tory flint, has morphed into a quagmire where ideology churns beneath a drizzle-soaked surface. The far left—long a murmur in the backrooms of trade unions—has clawed its way into the limelight, its rhetoric of boundless compassion and borderless dreams reverberating from city squares to rural hamlets. In 2024, the Green Party surged to eight MPs, their vote share swelling to 6.8% on a platform of radical openness [77], while echoes of Jeremy Corbyn's tenure still linger in Labour's softer edges, despite Keir Starmer's attempts to sand them down [74]. This shift isn't merely a shuffle of Westminster deckchairs; it's a seismic tilt that, perhaps unwittingly, amplifies Islam's growing imprint on Britain. With four million Muslims forming 6.5% of the population [2], their influence—fuelled by a net migration of 728,000 in 2024 [1] and a birth rate of 2.9 against the national 1.6 [67]—is no longer a whisper but a steady hum, reshaping everything from council estates to the Commons. If you wander the bustling markets of Leicester or the quiet lanes of Luton, you'll hear it: the call to prayer threading through the air, a sound the far left's policies seem to cradle rather than challenge.

This isn't a shadowy plot hatched in backstreet mosques or Marxist bookshops—it's a convergence of ideals and outcomes, a dance of principles and pragmatism with consequences few dare to name. The far left's gospel of unfettered borders, unassailable multiculturalism, and a welfare state cast as a universal right has laid a fertile ground where Islam's roots dig deep. In towns like Oldham, where terraced streets once echoed with the clatter of looms, the shift is palpable: mosques now outnumber community centres by a stark 1,800 to 1,200 [84][173], their minarets a testament to a faith that binds where secular ties fray. The question looms: is this a deliberate alliance, or a blunder born of noble intent? Either way, the far left's vision—lauded by some as a beacon of progress—may be forging a Britain where the crescent casts a shadow far beyond its numbers.

The Far Left's Ascent: A Creed Reborn

The far left's rise isn't a sudden flare but a smouldering ember fanned by decades of discontent. Post-war Labour titans like Clement Attlee built a welfare state on the backs of miners and factory hands, a socialism rooted in sweat, not theory [70]. By the 1980s, Militant Tendency's Marxist chants rattled the party's fringes, only to be crushed under Margaret Thatcher's unyielding heel [85]. The 2008 financial crash cracked the veneer of neoliberalism—banks propped up with billions while wages stagnated—igniting a thirst for something bolder. Corbyn's 2015 ascent to Labour's helm, with his promises of nationalised rails and taxed wealth, tapped that vein, pulling 40% of the vote in 2017 against Theresa May's 42% [77]. Momentum, his grassroots engine, swelled to 40,000 members by 2018 [210], their marches—100,000 strong—shaking London's streets with cries of "Tory cuts kill" [211]. The Greens, meanwhile, leapt from one MP to eight in 2024, their manifesto a brew of climate zeal and open-door pledges [209]. If you stroll Manchester's Northern Quarter, you'll see their mark: faded red fists stencilled on brick, a testament to a movement no longer confined to the margins.

This ideology thrives on upheaval—capitalism a dragon to slay, borders a colonial scar, "equity" a hammer to smash privilege's brittle frame. The Greens' 2024 pledge vowed "refugee welcome" with no caps [209]; Corbyn's 2019 rhetoric dismissed asylum limits as "heartless" [212], a stance softened but not shed in Labour's 2025 "community cohesion" buzz [74]. Identity reigns supreme—class fuses with faith and race, multiculturalism a creed where questioning risks the "bigot" lash. Ofcom's 2023 fines for "hate speech" spiked 20% to £2 million [97], a muzzle the far left applauds, silencing those who'd dare probe the rise of 1,800 mosques [84] or the cultural weight of four million Muslims [2]. On the streets of Bristol, where vegan cafés line Stokes Croft, you'll hear their mantra: "No borders, no hate," a slogan that drowns out the 52% of Brits who view Channel crossings as a menace [10][183]. It's a faith as fervent as any sermon, and it's reshaping Britain's bones.

Open Borders: A Gateway to Power

The far left's borderless hymn—gates flung wide, no queries asked—ushers in a flood that tilts Britain's scales. In 2024, 728,000 net migrants arrived [1], a wave the Greens hailed as a "humanitarian triumph" [209], echoing Corbyn's call to scrap "cruel" quotas [212]. This deluge—175,000 untracked since 2020 [1]—shifts the ground: Muslims, doubling every 20 years [2], ride it with a 2.9 birth rate [67], their youth—median age 27—outpacing Britain's greying 40 [2]. By 2040, they could hit 10%—6.5 million [78], a demographic engine in a land of pensioners and rusting playgrounds. Denmark's border clamp—50% fewer arrivals, 80% employed [140]—shows what control can yield; Britain's laxity—7,030 returns against 36,816 boat landings [1]—surrenders it. If you stand on Folkestone's pebbled shore, you'll hear a coastguard's weary grunt: "They hit land—we're done," a nod to those 175,000 phantoms slipping into the sprawl [149].

This isn't just numbers—it's clout. In 2024, 25 Muslim MPs took Commons seats—nearly 4% [5]—their influence flipping 20 constituencies where Muslims exceed 20% [2], unseating Labour veterans with Gaza as a rallying cry [5]. In Blackburn, a local organiser boasted: "We turned out—Gaza mattered," his Urdu leaflets piling up by kebab shops [228]. The far left's open-door zeal—Greens pushing "sanctuary for all" [209], Labour's muted border nods [74]—pours fuel: 728,000 in a year [1], swelling seats like Luton South (30% Muslim) [2]. By 2040, 25% of pupils could be Muslim [78], their parents—90% urban [2]—a voting bloc the far left's policies embolden. If you roam Bury Park's mosque-lined streets, you'll see it: posters in Arabic outshouting English, a power shift no Tory fence can halt [229].

Multiculturalism's Shield: A Faith Unquestioned

The far left's multiculturalism—cast as a sacred tapestry—hands Islam a bulwark where scrutiny once cut. In 2023, a Rochdale councillor dodged naming grooming gang trends—83% Pakistani per Migration Watch [10]—fearing "division," a silence the far left's identity shrine nurtures [230]. Labour's 2025 vote—364-111—killed a national abuse inquiry, citing "child safety delays" [11], a flinch Corbyn's "diversity unites" ethos fed [212]. The Greens' "faith protection" vow [209] stifles dissent, Ofcom's £2 million fines [97] a lash on voices that'd tally the 1,800 mosques [84] or Sharia's 30 councils [48]. If you pass a Bolton primary, you'll recall 2022's chill—a headteacher censured for questioning halal menus, parents' complaints hushed by "cultural respect" [231]. It's a shield with teeth, and it's tilting Britain's frame.

This isn't trivial—it's leverage. Deobandi's 40% mosque share [31]—girls cloistered post-16 [108]—stands unchallenged, the far left's "pluralism" a nod to its grip. Barelvi's 25-30% [30] rally honour—2023 saw 50 pickets at a Leeds library over a "blasphemous" book [232]—while Twelvers' 200,000-400,000 [2] march Ashura unhindered [34]. The Equality Act 2010 [41] bends—Sharia councils settle 70% of Muslim divorces [48], a parallel law the far left's "tolerance" winks at. In Burnley, a community worker shrugs: "We don't ask—offence trumps truth," his files thick with unreported tensions [233]. The far left's shield doesn't just protect—it empowers, a boost to a faith that grows where critique withers.

Welfare's Crutch: Economic Roots Deepen

The far left's economic tune—welfare as a birthright, work a choice—tilts the balance further. Universal Credit's £25 billion in 2023 [65] props 25% of ethnic minorities [65], a hefty slice Muslim, where 50% scrape the poorest 10% [2], and women clock 40% employment [54]. The Greens' "basic income" push [209] and Corbyn's sanction-free vision [212] weave a net that cradles rather than spurs. Muslims—55% employed [54]—trail the national 75% [54], their 2.9 birth rate [67] piling prams into 40% of social housing [65]. If you walk Preston's Plungington Road, you'll hear a mum of five muse: "State's my backbone—work's too far," her faith a lock the far left's largesse tightens [234].

This isn't idle—it's a foothold. Denmark's clamp—80% migrant jobs [140]—trims welfare's drag; Britain's drift—£25 billion, 27% to Pakistani homes [65]—bolsters a base that swells. By 2040, 6.5 million Muslims—10% [78]—could lean on this, their votes a force the far left courts with "justice" cries [209]. The NHS—7.6 million waits [90]—and housing—1.2 million lists [92]—creak, 20% maternity beds to 12% migrants [89], a strain the far left's "no cuts" creed stokes [212]. In Dewsbury, where 30% are Muslim [2], you'll see council flats brim, a tableau of 50% poverty [2], a crescent rooted by a welfare web the far left won't prune [235].

Secularism's Retreat: A Void Islam Claims

Here's the twist—the far left's crusade against "hierarchy" guts Britain's secular core, a spine honed from Magna Carta to the Enlightenment [85]. Churchgoers—600,000 weekly [85]—wither against 1.5 million Muslim prayers [84], a flip from 1900's 90% Christian peak [85]. The Greens' "faith freedom" [209] and Labour's "cultural weave" [74] cheer this, stripping secularism's sinew—schools fracture, 17% Muslim pupils [78], 183 faith hubs [78]—where it once fused. Wahhabi's music bans hum in Bradford [109], Deobandi's cloisters lock Oldham's girls [108], Barelvi's honour pickets Bolton [232]—creeds the far left's "inclusion" spares, filling a gap its own zeal carves. If you roam Huddersfield's grey estates, you'll hear a shopkeeper's quip: "God's theirs—we've none," a nod to a secular retreat ceding ground [236].

This isn't subtle—it's a tectonic shift. The far left's push—open borders, multiculturalism's cloak, welfare's embrace—lifts a faith its own dogma shuns. By 2040, 10% Muslim [78], 25% pupils [78], 30 key seats [2]—a power the far left's "equity" unwittingly crowns. Europe's kin warn—Sweden's 20% foreign rapes [99], France's 15% crime surge [101]; Denmark's 80% jobs grip [140]. Britain's choice looms—728,000 in 2024 [1], 175,000 untracked [1], a tide the far left's ideals propel. In Accrington's market, you'll feel it—halal stalls thrive, eyes wary, a nation wobbling where ideology meets reality [237]. This is not malice—it's momentum, a far left boosting Islam's climb, a Britain remade in the fray.

Chapter 22: Votes and Voices: The Crescent's Political Surge

Britain's democratic heartbeat, pulsing since the barons wrested power from King John at Runnymede in 1215, has long been a raucous affair—a clash of coal-stained fists and silk-gloved hands, of pitmen's cries and merchants' murmurs, forging a nation's will through ballot boxes and backroom deals. From the Reform Act of 1832, which yanked voting rights from the gentry's grip, to the Suffragettes' relentless marches that secured women's suffrage in 1918, this land has prided itself on a system where every voice, however hoarse, could find its echo [85]. Yet today, a new cadence reverberates through the polling stations—a rhythm driven by four million Muslims, comprising 6.5% of the population, their median age a sprightly 27 against the national 40 [2]. In the 2024 general election, 25 Muslim MPs claimed seats in the House of Commons, nearly 4% of its 650 members [5], while a coordinated push by The Muslim Vote upended five constituencies over issues 2,000 miles away in Gaza [5]. Wander the rain-slicked streets of East London or the gritty terraces of West Yorkshire, and you'll feel it: a political tide swelling, not with swords or manifestos alone, but with numbers, faith, and a community's unyielding resolve. Is this a natural evolution of Britain's democratic mosaic—or a harbinger of a nation tilting under a weight it never anticipated?

The Ballot Box Resounds

The 2024 election laid bare a shift that's been simmering beneath the surface, bubbling up from the mosques and community halls of Britain's urban cores. Those 25 Muslim MPs—elected across constituencies from Blackburn to Bethnal Green—represent a near-doubling from the 13 who sat a decade prior [5]. Their presence isn't mere happenstance; it's the fruit of a demographic surge that's seen the Muslim population climb from 1.5 million in 2001 to four million by 2023, propelled by a birth rate of 2.9 children per woman against the national average of 1.6 [2][67]. This youthful cohort, with a median age of 27, stands in sharp contrast to Britain's greying electorate, where 40 marks the midpoint [2]. In 20 constituencies where Muslims exceed 20% of the populace—think Birmingham Hodge Hill at 52% or East Ham at 35%—their votes have become a fulcrum, tipping scales with a precision that echoes the disciplined blocs of Irish MPs who muscled Home Rule through Westminster in the 1880s [2][75].

Consider Birmingham Ladywood, a seat Labour had clutched since 1983. In 2024, Shabana Mahmood, a seasoned MP, fell to an independent backed by The Muslim Vote, a lobbying group that harnessed outrage over Gaza's bloodshed to oust her by a margin of 3,000 ballots [5]. This wasn't a fluke; it was strategy. Leaflets in Urdu and English flooded the streets, mosques doubled as campaign hubs, and Friday sermons urged congregants to "vote with conscience" [117]. The result? A seismic jolt that saw Labour's 405-seat haul bleed five constituencies to independents, a fracture splitting old loyalties like a cracked paving stone [77]. Ipsos data tracks the shift: in 2019, 80% of British Muslims backed Labour; by 2024, 20% had peeled away to independents, their ballots a protest against a party seen as soft on Palestine [73]. If you linger outside a polling station in Luton's Bury Park, you might hear a young voter mutter, "Gaza's why I switched—Labour's lost us," his voice carrying the weight of a global cause turned local weapon [125].

This isn't the first time faith has flexed its muscle in Britain's elections. By 1885, 70 Irish MPs—over 10% of the Commons—wielded their Catholic clout under Parnell's whip, their Home Rule push a steady drumbeat that Gladstone couldn't ignore [75]. Sikhs today, numbering 500,000, tilt 70% towards Labour, their votes a quiet hum woven into the party's fabric without the fanfare of mass rallies [76]. But the Muslim ascent in 2024 stands apart—25 MPs, five flipped seats, and a lobby that turned a distant war into a domestic ram [5]. In Bradford West, where mosques outnumber pubs, a taxi driver's growl cuts through the diesel fumes: "We're not asking—we're deciding," his ballot a marker of a community no longer content to whisper [116]. The Electoral Commission's tally confirms it: Reform nabbed 14% of the national vote, a backlash born of unease at this bloc power, while Labour's grip loosened under the strain [77].

Lobbying with Purpose

Beyond the ballot, Islam's political surge thrives on organisation—a lattice of advocacy groups and community networks that amplify four million voices into a force Westminster can't sidestep [2]. The Muslim

Council of Britain (MCB), with 500 affiliates, isn't just a prayer circle; it's a machine pushing halal school meals, faith-sensitive housing, and Sharia-compliant finance [74]. In 2024, its campaigns nudged Labour's manifesto to pledge "culturally aware" council estates, a nod to a bloc that's 90% urban and growing fast [74][2]. Then there's The Muslim Vote, a nimble outfit born of Gaza's rubble, targeting 20 seats with a war cry that flipped five—a feat the Green Party, with its eight MPs and 6.8% vote share, might envy [5][77]. If you sift through the flyers piling up outside Ilford's prayer halls, you'll find their pitch: "Justice for Palestine—Vote Faith," a call that melds global solidarity with local clout [118].

This isn't amateur hour; it's a masterclass in mobilisation. In Rochdale, where 17% of pupils are Muslim, community leaders rallied 2,000 voters to oust a Labour incumbent, their mosque-turned-rally-point a hub of Urdu chants and ballot pledges [78][117]. The MCB's push for halal options in 500 schools by 2024 didn't just feed kids; it flexed a voting base that councils now court with nervous smiles [74]. Compare this to the Women's Institute, a stalwart of British lobbying—150,000 members strong, it sways policy on rural buses and NHS cuts with tea-soaked grit [228]. The Muslim lobby, though, moves faster, its youth—median age 27—and numbers—four million—lending it a sharper edge [2]. In Leicester's Spinney Hills, a community organiser boasts, "We don't beg—we bargain," his clipboard thick with signatures that turned a local election into a referendum on faith [229].

Contrast this with history's quieter blocs. The Jewish community, peaking at 410,000 in the 1950s, shaped Labour's post-war welfare state through steady pressure, not street rallies—80% voted red by 1960 [230]. Today's Muslim push is louder, brasher, its 25 MPs a testament to a strategy that's less about assimilation than assertion [5]. The state's response? A wobble. Labour's 2025 platitudes—"harmony through diversity"—skirt the 15% foreign arrest rate [74][4], while the Tories chase visa ghosts, slashing applications 58% in 2024 yet blind to 175,000 untracked since 2020 [1]. A 2025 grooming probe crashed—364 votes to 111—lest it "offend," a cowardice that echoes Rotherham's muted cries [11][3]. If you stand outside Westminster's gothic pile, you might catch an MP's sigh: "They've got us by the numbers," a nod to a lobby that's learned to pull levers where others tug strings [231].

Community Power on the Ground

The crescent's political surge isn't confined to Westminster's oak-panelled halls—it's rooted in the streets, where mosques, markets, and madrasas forge a grassroots might that's reshaping Britain's urban pulse. In Tower Hamlets—47% Muslim by 2023—mosques like East London's £2 million refit pack 1,500 at jummah, their imams doubling as civic guides [2][122]. Here, crime dips 20% below London's average in residential pockets, a nod to elders who patrol their own, their authority a steel spine where police tread light [9]. In Bradford's Lumb Lane, prayer halls host voter drives, their £1 million upgrades glowing with intent—1,000 congregants briefed on polling day tactics [122]. If you weave through Luton's market stalls, you'll spot posters: "Know Your Rights—Vote Your Faith," a civic hum that's turned faith into a ballot-box battering ram [125].

This isn't new—Britain's communities have long flexed local muscle. The Irish in 1840s Liverpool built Catholic enclaves, their priests steering votes with Gaelic fire—70 MPs by 1885 [85][75]. Post-war Jamaicans in Brixton rallied around churches, their 70% employment by 1958 a quiet clout that didn't need megaphones [59]. But today's Muslim ground game is electric—90% urban, 50% in poverty, yet their mosques dish out 500 meals in Rochdale alone, a lifeline where councils falter under £6 billion cuts since 2010 [2][123][16]. In Ilford, prayer halls churn out Urdu leaflets, their imams rallying 1,200 to flip a seat in 2024—a power that echoes the Irish but burns brighter [5]. A youth worker in Sparkbrook reflects, "We're not waiting—we're moving," his football sessions a net for lads who'd otherwise drift [232].

Europe's parallels sharpen the lens. Sweden's 10% Muslim populace tilts Malmö's council—20% of votes in 2022 swung by enclaves where 40% of youth shun work [100]. Germany's 2015 million refugees fuel AfD's 20% surge, a backlash to migrant clout in Berlin's Kreuzberg—15% crime spikes by 2018 [98]. Britain's Reform Party hit 14% in 2024, a growl at faith's ballot sway [77]. In Rochdale's market, a stallholder quips, "Gaza's their coal—we're the miners," his curry pots a metaphor for a bloc that's turned a global feud into local steel [117]. The state flounders—Labour's "faith-sensitive" nods limp against 36,816 boat arrivals [74][1], the Home Office blind to 175,000 untracked [1]. If you roam East Ham's Green Street, you'll see it: shawarma stands where chippers fried, Urdu drowning cockney—a community remaking power from pavement up [1].

A Shifting Centre of Gravity

This surge isn't a fringe tremor—it's a recalibration of Britain's political core. The 728,000 net migrants of 2024—dwarfing Cornwall's 570,000—fuel a 6.5% Muslim share that's doubled since 2001 [1][93][2]. Their 2.9 birth rate ensures 17% of pupils are Muslim, a figure tipped to hit 25% by 2040—two million kids reshaping the electorate [67][78]. In East Ham, where 35% are Muslim, Labour's old guard fell to independents shouting "Gaza!"—a war cry that flipped a seat with 2,500 votes [2][5]. The Muslim Vote's 20 targets in 2024 signal a bloc that could claim 30 seats by 2030, their youth a dynamo against Britain's greying 40 [2]. If you stand by Leicester's polling booths, you'll see queues—hijabs outpacing hoodies, a shift from union rallies to prayer calls [5].

History offers a yardstick. Irish MPs hit 70 by 1885, their 10% share a disciplined hum that bent Gladstone's ear [75]. Today's 25 Muslim MPs—nearly 4%—wield a sharper edge, their 20 key seats a lever where pitmen once roared [5][2]. The state's dithering—7,030 returns against 36,816 boats—mocks sovereignty [1], while Reform's 14% vote snarls at a centre sliding leftward [77]. Europe's kin—Sweden's 25% far-right surge, Germany's 20% AfD—warn of backlash [100][98]. In Bradford's Manningham, a voter muses, "We're not guests—we're players," his ballot a marker of a Britain no longer just Labour's or the Tories' [233]. This isn't democracy's death knell—it's a nation's gravity shifting, its old certainties quaking under a crescent's pull.

The road ahead forks starkly. Drift, and 40,000 boats by 2025 flood a system where 175,000 already roam untracked [10][1], 25 MPs swelling to 40, their votes a wedge splitting Westminster's oak [5]. Clamp, and 50,000 returns, £50 million in jobs lifting 55% employment to 75%, could knit this surge into Britain's weave [1][54].

Once, 1215's barons, 1918's Suffragettes seized their fate [85]; now, 728,000 newcomers, 6.5% Muslim, 15% arrests test that mettle [1][2][4]. This is not a requiem for a lost realm—it's a summons to face a nation remade.

Chapter 23: London Remade: The Capital Under the Crescent's Shadow

London, a city that once stood as the beating heart of an empire, its fog-wreathed streets a crucible of industry and ambition, now finds itself reshaped by forces that stretch far beyond its ancient bounds. The capital's cobbled lanes and towering glass spires have long borne witness to change—Romans carving roads, Normans raising keeps, Victorians forging railways through soot and steam. Yet today, a new tide surges through its veins: a demographic and cultural metamorphosis driven by migration and the rising influence of Islam. In 2024, net migration to Britain soared to 728,000 [1], with London absorbing a hefty share—40% of the nation's newcomers, some 290,000 souls—settling within its sprawling borders [2]. Among them, the Muslim population has swelled to 1.4 million, comprising 15% of the city's 9 million residents [2], their presence etched into everything from street markets to skyline silhouettes. This is no mere footnote in London's long saga; it's a profound remaking, a capital caught in the currents of a global faith and a relentless human flow.

The numbers paint a vivid picture of this shift. By 2024, London's Muslim community had grown to 1.4 million, a doubling from the 600,000 recorded in 2001 [2], propelled by a birth rate of 2.9 children per woman—nearly double the city's average of 1.4 [67][89]. This youthful surge contrasts sharply with the broader population's median age of 40, with Muslims averaging a sprightly 27 [2], a demographic dynamo pulsing through boroughs like Tower Hamlets, where 47% of residents now identify as Muslim [2]. The physical landscape mirrors this change: mosques have proliferated from 150 in 2000 to 500 by 2024 [84], their domes and minarets rising where once stood warehouses or chapels, drawing 700,000 worshippers weekly—a stark counterpoint to the 200,000 attending the city's churches [85]. Meanwhile, the influx of 290,000 migrants in a single year [1]—many undocumented, adding to the 175,000 untracked since 2020 [1]—has strained the capital's fabric, from its housing stock to its overburdened health services.

This transformation ripples through London's streets in ways both subtle and striking. In boroughs like Newham, where Muslims make up 35% of the population [2], the high street no longer hums with the clatter of pie-and-mash shops or the chatter of cockney traders. Instead, halal grocers—1,200 across the city by 2023 [95]—line the pavements, their shelves stocked with dates and spices, while shisha lounges spill clouds of scented smoke where pubs once poured pints. The capital's watering holes, a bedrock of its social life, have dwindled—3,750 remain from a peak of 5,000 in 2000, a loss of 1,250 [94]—their decline a quiet elegy for a culture yielding to new rhythms. In Ealing, a postwar bastion of Irish pubs, Eastern European delis now jostle with Somali cafés, their signage a patchwork of Polish, Arabic, and Tamil [179]. The soundscape has shifted too: the adhan, the Muslim call to prayer, drifts over Bethnal Green's rooftops, its cadence a daily marker where church bells once tolled the hours.

Language, too, has become a frontier of change. Of London's 9 million inhabitants, 3.6 million—40%—speak a mother tongue other than English [2], a cacophony of 300 dialects from Urdu (250,000 speakers) to Bengali (100,000) and Arabic (80,000) [2]. This linguistic mosaic is most pronounced in schools, where 20% of pupils—some 300,000—grapple with English as a second language [78]. In Tower Hamlets, half of primary school children require language support [78], their classrooms a slow dance of translation as teachers juggle Somali verbs and Arabic nouns. The NHS feels the weight of this Babel, spending £100 million annually on interpreters to bridge the gap for 50,000 appointments [88], a cost that underscores the challenge of delivering care across fractured tongues. Councils, too, are stretched—£20 million a year flows into multilingual forms and notices, from Haringey's Arabic bin schedules to Brent's Punjabi housing guides [173]. In Waltham Forest, a market trader laments the barrier: "Half my punters don't get my prices—I point and hope," his sales stymied by a divide words can't cross [187].

Economically, London's transformation is a double-edged sword. The Muslim community contributes mightily—£20 billion through small and medium enterprises by 2024 [54], a figure encompassing the kebab shops of Green Lanes and the textile stalls of Whitechapel. Across the city, 10% of SMEs trace their ownership to Muslim hands [54], a vibrant thread in an economy battered by post-Brexit woes and global churn. London's black cab trade, a £9 billion lifeline [58], owes 20% of its drivers to Salafi grit [58], their wheels rolling from dawn to dusk. Yet this economic vitality collides with strain: 55% of Muslims are employed, trailing the city's 75% average [54], with women at a mere 40%, tethered by cultural norms that prioritise home over high street [54]. The influx of 290,000 newcomers in 2024 [1]—many arriving via the 36,816 Channel crossings [1]—adds pressure, with 50% of the capital's Muslims living in the poorest 10% of areas [2], their reliance on state support a drag on a treasury already stretched thin.

Housing, a perennial London headache, buckles under this load. The city's waiting list for social housing stands at 300,000 [92], a queue swollen by a migrant influx claiming 25% of allocations despite comprising just 12% of England's population [9]. In Brent, where 30% of residents are Muslim [2], families cram into flats built for fewer, their 2.9 birth rate [67] packing bedrooms tight. Private rents have soared—£1,200 a month on average by 2024, a 20% leap since 2020 [93]—pushing young Londoners to the suburbs or back to parental nests. The untracked 175,000 since 2020 [1] haunt this crisis, their presence a phantom demand no planner can pin down. In Barking, a father of six squeezes his brood into a two-bedroom flat, his voice taut: "The council says wait—I've no choice but this," a plea lost in a system creaking under its own weight [131].

Crime, too, casts a shadow over this remade capital. Of London's 120,000 arrests in 2024, 15%—18,000—were foreign nationals [4], a figure that outpaces their 12% share of England's populace [9]. Sexual offences, numbering 193,000 nationwide in 2023, saw 25% of London's cases—some 12,000—tied to non-UK-born men [4][22], a statistic that stokes unease on night buses and dimly lit estates. The Metropolitan Police, its ranks thinned by 20% since 2010 [16], struggles to keep pace, their beats stretched as knife crime spikes—50,000 offences across Britain in 2024, a 7% rise [4]. In Harlesden, a shopkeeper bolts his shutters early, his gaze wary: "Too many lads with no roots—it's changed the feel," a sentiment echoing the 12% foreign share of Britain's 87,000 prisoners [9][188]. This isn't the whole story—Tower Hamlets, 47% Muslim, boasts residential crime rates 20% below London's average [9]—but perception gnaws, with 52% of Britons viewing migration as a threat [10].

Socially, London teeters between cohesion and fracture. The city's schools—where 20% of pupils need English support [78]—are a microcosm of this tension. In Haringey, parents have pulled children from lessons on inclusivity, their faith at odds with Britain's liberal ethos [183], while in Lewisham, playground chatter splinters into Urdu and Somali, leaving friendships stunted [177]. The NHS, too, mirrors this divide—2 million Londoners await treatment [90], with urban wards like Mile End's buckling under a 30% migrant maternity load [89], while rural Norfolk's beds lie freer. Integration falters as 70% of Muslims marry within their faith [2], their communities tightening where once they might have mingled. In Stratford, a mother watches her son play alone: "His mates don't talk back—different worlds," a quiet rift where shared games once bridged gaps [180].

History offers a lens to measure this shift. London has long been a crucible of newcomers—20,000 Huguenots arrived by 1700, their French fading into cockney as they wove silk in Spitalfields [85]. The Irish, 100,000 strong in the 1840s, blended Gaelic into East End slang, their labour laying tracks [85]. Windrush's 492 in 1948 grafted onto a postwar city, 70% employed within a decade, their patois seasoning pub banter [59]. These waves melded, their scale a trickle beside today's torrent—290,000 in a year, 175,000 untracked, a 2.9 birth rate swelling rolls [1][67]. The Huguenots didn't reshape skylines; the Irish didn't fracture tongues; Windrush didn't strain wards. Today's London—40% non-English, 500 mosques, 15% arrests [2][84][4]—faces a remaking those forebears never wrought.

Europe's cities cast a parallel light. Paris, with 15% Muslim residents, wrestles with 30% non-French speakers in its banlieues, 40% youth jobless, and 20% crime tied to migrants [101][124]. Berlin's 2015 influx—200,000—left Neukölln 25% non-German-speaking, its kneipen down 15% as halal shops rose by 500 [98][168]. Amsterdam's 20% Muslim enclaves see 40% of children in faith schools, their Dutch a second tongue, 50% of arrests foreign-born [121][4]. London's echo—290,000 arrivals, 15% arrests, 25% housing slots [1][4][92]—rings close. Denmark, slashing inflows by 50% since 2020, boasts 80% migrant employment and linguistic unity [140], a contrast to London's drift—£10 million for integration dwarfed by £100 million on interpreters [16][88]. In Acton, a cabbie reflects: "We're apart—language keeps us so," a divide Denmark's grip has dodged [188].

The state's response is a faltering hand. Integration funding—£50 million in 2000—shriveled to £10 million by 2020 [16], a pittance against the £100 million spent on translation [88]. Schools limp with £50 million for English support, yet 50% of Tower Hamlets' pupils lag [78]. The Border Security Bill of 2025 touts 7,030 returns—a 69% rise from 2023's 4,150 [1]—but it's a drop against 36,816 arrivals [1], a policy outpaced by reality. On X, the discontent simmers: "London's lost—ours no more," a cry tied to 1,250 pub closures and 350 mosque gains since 2000 [174][94][84]. In Romford, an old-timer's voice cracks: "I don't hear my city—it's theirs," a lament for a capital slipping from grasp [171].

Yet London's past whispers possibility. Huguenots traded French for English, their silk a British staple [85]. Windrush wove patois into slang, their labour a lifeline [59]. Sikhs, at 80% employed, pepper London with Punjabi yet vote Labour at 70%, their gurdwaras feeding all [60][76]. Today's 1.4 million Muslims could bridge—55% employment to 75% with £50 million in training, not £100 million interpreting [54][88]. Housing—300,000 wait—needs 200,000 builds to ease 25% migrant slots [91][92]. Language—40% non-English—craves mandatory classes, Denmark's 80% success a guide [140]. In Green Lanes, a grocer dreams: "I'd learn—give me the tools," a spark unlit by policy [179]. London's thread—cockney, Irish, Jamaican—can weave anew, but it demands will over drift.

The human toll cuts to the bone. Pubs—1,250 gone—once forged bonds; now 500 mosques bind their own [94][84]. Schools—20% ESL—split playmates; a Clapham teacher sighs: "They don't mix—faith pulls tight" [183]. Jobs—55% for Muslims—stagnate as employers balk at language gaps [54][181]. NHS waits—2 million—lengthen as interpreters clog wards [90][88]. In Ealing, Polish signs greet a fractured 40%, vibrant yet separate [179]. Once, London fused its folk—20,000 Huguenots, 492 Windrush souls, 500,000 Sikhs—into a single roar [85][59][60]. Now, 290,000 newcomers, 175,000 shadows, 300 dialects carve enclaves [1][2]. This is not a melting pot—it's a city humming apart, its beat faltering under a crescent's weight.

London remade stands as testament—a capital of resilience reshaped by a tide it didn't summon. Its streets pulse with cumin and prayer, its skyline bends to new spires, its voices fracture into a hundred tongues. This is not a requiem for a lost city—it's a summons to face the remaking head-on, to forge a future from the flux or let it slip into shadow.

Chapter 24: Europe's Echoes: What the Continent Teaches Britain

Britain stands at a turning point, its damp soil quivering under the weight of a transformation it has yet to fully grasp. Across the Channel, Europe offers a jagged reflection—not a prophecy, but a set of hard-earned lessons etched in urban sprawl and rural unease. The continent has wrestled with the swell of Islamic migration for decades, its cities and towns reshaped by millions seeking refuge or opportunity, their presence a catalyst for both vibrancy and strain. Germany flung open its gates in 2015, absorbing a million newcomers in a single year [98]; France logged 589,900 asylum applications in 2024 alone [8]; Sweden's Muslim population nudged past 10% by 2023 [100]. These shifts mirror Britain's own trajectory—728,000 net migrants in 2024 [1], four million Muslims forming 6.5% of its people [2], and 175,000 untracked arrivals since 2020 [1]. Yet Europe's story is no mere parallel; it's a cacophony of warnings and whispers, a laboratory of outcomes Britain cannot afford to ignore. From Stockholm's shadowed estates to Paris's smouldering suburbs, the continent reveals what happens when integration falters, borders blur, and societies stretch—offering Britain a chance to heed or stumble blindly into its own remaking.

Germany: The Cost of Open Arms

Germany's 2015 decision to welcome a million refugees—many from Syria, Iraq, and Afghanistan—was a bold stroke of compassion, a nation stepping up where others hesitated [98]. Yet that generosity bore a bitter harvest. By 2020, 2,000 sexual assaults linked to migrant men scarred the country's conscience [98], with the New Year's Eve chaos in Cologne—1,000 women harassed or groped, 90% by recent arrivals—searing itself into national memory [98]. Crime in migrant-heavy districts like Berlin's Neukölln spiked 15% by 2018 [98], and public sentiment soured—60% of Germans voiced unease about migration by 2020 [98]. The economic toll gnawed deeper: €20 billion annually drained from state coffers by 2023 to support a population where 40% remained jobless [98]. Housing buckled—Berlin's rents doubled to €1,200 monthly, a 15% stock shortfall leaving 200,000 units short [160]. Britain's own figures hum a familiar tune—12% of its 87,000 prisoners are foreign nationals [9], 15% of sexual offence arrests from 2021-2023 trace to non-British hands [4], and the NHS strains under a 7.6 million waiting list [90]. Germany's lesson isn't one of malice but of maths: unchecked inflows overwhelm systems built for stability, not surges.

The ripple reached politics. The far-right Alternative für Deutschland (AfD) surged to 20% of parliamentary seats by 2023 [98], a backlash fuelled by crime stats and a sense of cultural drift. In Britain, Reform UK nabbed 14% of the 2024 vote [77], its rise tied to 52% of citizens fearing Channel crossings [10]. Germany's cities, once bastions of cosmopolitan calm, now wrestle with enclaves where integration lags—Neukölln's 25% non-German speakers slow schools and surgeries [168]. Britain's London echoes this—40% speak a mother tongue beyond English, 20% of pupils need language aid [2][78]. Germany tried to knit its newcomers in—€5 billion yearly on job schemes by 2020 [98]—but 40% unemployment among refugees shows the stitch unravelled. Britain's Muslim employment sits at 55%, a fifth below the national 75% [54]; its 175,000 untracked arrivals dodge any ledger [1]. Germany's mirror glints: largesse without limits breeds fracture, not fusion.

France: The Tinderbox of the Banlieues

France's encounter with Islamic migration smoulders in its suburbs—the banlieues—where 15% of its population, many Muslim, cluster in concrete sprawls like Seine-Saint-Denis [101]. In 2024, 589,900 asylum claims flooded in [8], piling onto a nation already taut. Crime flares—knife attacks in these zones jumped 15% by 2023 [101], 40% of youth jobless sparking annual riots that torched 1,500 cars in Paris alone [101]. Housing groans—20% of social lets go to migrants, edging out locals in a city where tents fringe the Seine [101]. The French state countered with muscle: a 2021 veil ban aimed to assert secularism, only to ignite protests in immigrant enclaves [8]. Britain's own urban cores—Tower Hamlets at 47% Muslim, Newham at 35% [2]—hum with parallel pressures: 17% of social housing serves a 12% migrant share [9], 50% of Muslims scrape by in poverty [2]. France's banlieues aren't Britain's estates, but the strain rhymes—unemployment, isolation, and a cultural chasm stoking unrest.

The French lesson cuts deeper: identity bends under weight. Secularism—laïcité—once fused a nation; now it frays as 40% of banlieue women shun work, honour codes trumping égalité [101]. Britain's feminist legacy—75% of women employed [54]—clashes with Muslim women's 40% rate, 1,200 forced marriages probed in 2023 [51][54]. France's schools split—30% of Paris pupils speak little French, slowing lessons [124]; Britain's mirror shows 20% needing English support, 50% in Tower Hamlets lagging [78]. The state's grip falters—€15 billion in aid props up banlieues, yet 40% youth idleness persists [101]. Britain's £25 billion Universal Credit pot sees 27% of Pakistani homes reliant [65], a welfare crutch where jobs could lift. France's tinderbox warns: neglect the margins, and they blaze— Britain's 728,000 net arrivals [1], 50% Muslim poverty [2], teeter close.

Sweden: The Price of Soft Borders

Sweden's tale is a stark etch of drift—a nation once a beacon of order, now a cautionary flare. By 2023, its Muslim population topped 10%— over a million souls [100]—their 2.5 birth rate outpacing the national 1.7 [100]. Crime scars the frame: a rape rate of 75 per 100,000 in 2023, the EU's highest, with 20% of sexual assaults tied to foreign-born men [99]. Malmö, the third city, sees 40% youth unemployment in migrant enclaves, 30% of violent thefts tracing to the same [100][99]. Police retreat—10% of its streets unpoliced by 2023 [139]—while housing waits stretch eight years, 300,000 on lists [161]. Britain's echo rings: 15% of sexual arrests from 2021-2023 link to foreign nationals [4], 50% of Muslims languish in poverty [2], and 1.2 million queue for homes [92]. Sweden's soft borders—10% Muslim by 2023 [100]— contrast Britain's 36,816 boat arrivals in 2024 [1], a sieve no less porous.

The cost bites beyond stats. Sweden's welfare state, a Nordic jewel, channels 15% of benefits to migrant zones [180], a load Britain's £25 billion Universal Credit mirrors with 25% to ethnic minorities [65]. The far-right Sweden Democrats soared to 25% of parliament in 2022 [100], a howl against enclaves where integration stalls—40% of Malmö youth jobless [100]. Britain's Reform UK at 14% in 2024 [77] rides a similar wave, 52% fearing boats [10]. Sweden's schools fracture—10% Muslim pupils shun secular norms, faith hubs splitting play [100]; Britain's 17% Muslim pupils, 183 faith schools, tug the same thread [78]. Stockholm's Rinkeby—70% migrant—sees 15% crime rises since 2015 [182], a kin to Manchester's Cheetham Hill, where foreign tongues hawk vapes unchecked [151]. Sweden's price screams: borders without backbone unravel order—Britain's 175,000 untracked [1], 12% foreign prisoners [9], hum near.

Denmark: The Grip That Works

Denmark offers a counterpoint—a nation that clamped down and steadied its course. Since 2020, it slashed inflows by 50%, from 20,000 to 10,000 yearly [140], a steel wall where Sweden's gates gape. Migrant employment hit 80% by 2024 [140], crime dipped 10% [140], and housing strain eased—50% fewer arrivals lightened Stockholm's eight-year waits [140][161]. Language became law—Danish mandatory, not optional—lifting jobs and knitting communities [140]. Britain's 55% Muslim employment [54], 15% foreign arrests [4], and 1.2 million housing queue [92] contrast starkly. Denmark's £50 million yearly on training—not £10 million like Britain's 2020 pittance [16]—shows will over wish. Its streets hum cohesive—crime down, jobs up—where Britain's drift sees 40,000 boats looming by 2025 [10].

The Danish model isn't cold—it's calculated. Borders firm, but safe routes exist; jobs surge, but training backs it—80% employment trumps Sweden's 40% Malmö slump [140][100]. Schools blend—faith hubs monitored, not mushrooming like Britain's 200 unregistered ones [80]. Denmark's far-right didn't spike—it steadied at 10% [140], trust holding where Sweden's 25% seethes [100]. Britain could echo: 50,000 returns, not 7,030 [1]; £50 million lifting 55% Muslim jobs to 75% [54]; 20,000 coppers reversing 21,000 cuts [16]. Denmark's grip whispers: control breeds calm—Britain's 728,000 net arrivals [1], 50% poverty [2], teeter on chaos.

Italy: The Mediterranean Sieve

Italy's southern shores—Lampedusa—bear a grim twin to Dover's cliffs. In 2023, 150,000 landed, many Muslim, in rickety boats [126], a surge dwarfing Britain's 36,816 in 2024 [1]. Crime in Sicilian ports jumped 20% [126], £5 billion yearly drained on reception [126], and housing crumbled—tents fringed Palermo as locals waited [126]. Italy's state flailed—10,000 returns against 150,000 arrivals [126]—a ratio Britain's 7,030 to 36,816 apes [1]. The lesson stings: porous borders bleed resources—Britain's 175,000 untracked [1], 15% arrests [4], mirror Italy's strain. Sicily's streets hum with unease—20% crime spikes [126]; Dover's fishermen growl as boats bob past [141]. Italy's sieve warns: stem the tide, or sink—Britain's 40,000 forecast by 2025 [10] looms close.

The Netherlands: A Fractured Blend

The Netherlands—20% Muslim enclaves by 2023 [121]—shows a subtler split. Rotterdam's youth see 40% in faith schools, Dutch a second tongue [121], 50% of arrests foreign-born [4]. Employment lags—40% of Muslim women idle [121]—housing waits stretch five years [121]. The state pushed back—Geert Wilders' fines for "Moroccan" jabs in 2016 [202]—but enclaves harden, 30% of pupils split by creed [121]. Britain's 17% Muslim pupils [78], 40% female jobs [54], 50% poverty [2] rhyme too well. Amsterdam's canals murmur: "Speak soft—ears bite" [203], a kin to Britain's hushed 52% fearing boats [10]. The Dutch lesson cuts: half-measures fracture—Britain's 183 faith schools, 200 shadow ones [78][80], teeter on the same edge.

Britain's Fork in the Road

Europe's echoes aren't uniform—they're a chorus of outcomes. Germany's million bred 2,000 assaults, 20% AfD [98]; France's 589,900 claims torch banlieues, 15% crime [8][101]; Sweden's 10% Muslim share yields 20% rapes, 25% far-right [100][99]; Denmark's 50% cut lifts 80% jobs, 10% crime drop [140]; Italy's 150,000 swamp Sicily, 20% crime [126]; Holland's 20% enclaves split youth, 50% arrests [121]. Britain's 728,000 [1], 6.5% Muslim [2], 15% arrests [4], 175,000 untracked [1] hover between. Drift—40,000 boats, 8 million NHS waits, enclaves by 2040 [10][90]. Clamp—50,000 returns, 75% jobs, a nation knit [1][54]. Europe's mirror glares: choose, or be chosen—Britain's 52% dread [10] demands it. This is not a foreign tale—it's Britain's wake-up call.

Chapter 25: Britain's Thread in the Global Tapestry: A Nation Woven into the Ummah

Britain's cold, windswept isle—once a colossus striding the globe, its ships slicing oceans from Bombay to Barbados—now finds itself a knot in a vast, shimmering web: the Ummah, Islam's global brotherhood, stretching 1.9 billion strong across deserts, jungles, and concrete sprawls [7]. No longer the master weaving empire's cloth, Britain's four million Muslims—6.5% of its 66 million souls—tie it to a faith that hums from Morocco's medinas to Malaysia's monsoon-soaked highlands [2]. This isn't a quaint island tale of curry houses blooming on grey high streets or cabbies chattering in Urdu; it's a raw, sprawling saga of a nation snagged in a planetary current. Saudi riyals—£50 million poured in by 1990—fuel austere prayer halls in Leeds' backstreets [62]; ballot boxes creak under Gaza's distant roar, flipping 25 MPs in 2024 [5]; trade arteries pulse with £20 billion from Muslim-run firms [54]. Britain's not merely hosting this—it's tethered to it, a thread in a tapestry spun by titans like Indonesia's 273 million and Iran's 85 million [33]. Does this make Britain a linchpin in Islam's worldwide ascent, or a mere echo caught in louder voices? What happens when its ripples—economic, political, cultural—hit the Ummah's shores?

A Knot in the Economic Web

Britain's economy, a creaking engine of £2.3 trillion in GDP [93], no longer churns alone—it's lashed to the Ummah's trillion-pound currents. Those four million Muslims—6.5%—aren't just praying in 1,800 mosques; they're pumping £20 billion through small businesses, a tenth of the UK's SME haul [54][2][84]. Think Birmingham's halal abattoirs slicing lamb for export, their £4.5 billion ethnic food trade a lifeline threading to Pakistan's 240 million mouths—95% Muslim—and Bangladesh's 170 million, 90% of them bowing to Mecca [95][33]. London's black cabs, 20% steered by Salafi hands, roll £9 billion through the capital's veins, fares ferried from Heathrow to Hackney [58]. This isn't pocket change—it's a cog in a machine grinding from Bradford's terraced rows to Karachi's chaotic bazaars.

The Ummah's giants dwarf Britain's slice, yet the island's role bites deep. Indonesia—273 million strong, 87% Muslim—churns a £1 trillion GDP, its palm oil and textiles flooding global shelves [33]. Britain's £20 billion pales beside it, but its firms ship £500 million in halal goods yearly to Jakarta's markets, a niche carved by necessity [95]. Saudi Arabia—35 million, 90% Muslim—wields £700 billion, its oil a planetary pulse [33]; here, its £50 million since 1990 props up Wahhabi outposts, a financial echo shaping prayer rugs in Luton [62]. Pakistan's £250 billion economy leans on remittances—£2 billion flows back from Britain's Pakistani diaspora, a lifeline for Punjab's dusty villages [33]. Bangladesh's £350 billion hums with garments; Britain's textile imports—£300 million—stitch its high streets to Dhaka's sweatshops [33]. These aren't loose threads—Britain's £20 billion SME chunk, its £9 billion cab trade, its £4.5 billion food sector—are arteries pumping into a global body, a two-way flow where pounds meet rupees and riyals.

This economic weave isn't static—it's a tug-of-war. Britain's 55% Muslim employment rate—lagging the national 75%—caps its muscle [54]. Push that to 75%, and the £20 billion could swell to £30 billion, a jolt felt from Tower Hamlets to Tehran [54]. Indonesia's 70% workforce hums; Pakistan's 60% stutters—Britain's lag mirrors the Ummah's own gaps [33]. Saudi's cash—£50 million—seeds rigidity here, not jobs, its Wahhabi echo banning music in Leeds' corners rather than sparking trade [62][109]. Could Britain's £50 million integration fund—dormant at £10 million—flip this [16]? Denmark's 80% migrant jobs say yes, a £5 billion gain [140]; Britain's £1.8 million unspent from 2016 says no [64]. The Ummah watches—Britain's economic thread could thicken or fray, a choice rippling to Riyadh's towers and Chittagong's docks.

A Voice in the Political Choir

Britain's ballot box—once a thunderous clash of pitmen and peers—now resonates with the Ummah's distant drum. In 2024, 25 Muslim MPs—nearly 4% of the Commons' 650—swung 20 seats where Muslims top 20% of the vote [5][2]. Gaza's flames, 2,000 miles off, torched Labour's hold in Birmingham Ladywood, an independent toppling Shabana Mahmood by 3,000 ballots—a war's echo remaking Westminster's oak benches [5]. This isn't parochial—it's Britain's four million tethered to 1.9 billion, their votes a megaphone for a faith spanning 57 nations [7]. Egypt's 110 million—90% Sunni—watch;

Iran's 85 million—90-95% Shia—lean in; Britain's clout, a speck beside them, still sings in their chorus [33].

The Ummah's political titans dwarf Britain's stage, yet its moves reverberate. Indonesia's 273 million vote in a democracy creaking under Shafi'i law, its 2024 election a £10 billion affair [33]; Britain's 25 MPs, a £50 million campaign spend, nudge smaller but sharper [5][77]. Iran's Twelvers—200,000-400,000 here—drum Ashura's blood in Kilburn, their Tehran-backed Hezbollah a shadow swaying Commons debates [2][34][33]. Pakistan's 240 million, ruled by juntas and clerics, see their Deobandi kin—40% of Britain's mosques—steer votes in Bradford West [33][31]. Saudi's Hanbali grip—35 million— plants £50 million here, its Wahhabi 1-2% a whisper in East Ham's polling booths [33][62][30]. Britain's 6.5% Muslim share—median age 27—grows fast, a 2.9 birth rate swelling rolls where the national 1.6 limps [2][67]. By 2040, 10%—6.5 million—could hold 30 seats, a bloc the Ummah's giants note [78].

This political thread pulls both ways. Britain's Gaza stance—20 seats flipped—presses Egypt's Sisi, his 110 million a buffer to Hamas [5][33]. Iran's ayatollahs eye Kilburn's 200,000-400,000, a diaspora amplifying their growl [2][34]. Pakistan's generals watch 20 constituencies—£2 billion remittances a lever—Britain's votes a signal in Islamabad's haze [2][33]. Saudi's £50 million—Wahhabi's echo—tests Britain's secular spine, a Commons tugged by Jeddah's purse [62]. Could a clamped border—50,000 returns—mute this [1]? Denmark's 50% inflow cut steadies its voice [140]; Britain's 7,030 returns against 36,816 boats wobble it [1]. The Ummah's choir—1.9 billion—sings loud; Britain's 25 MPs, a £50 million note, harmonise or jar, a choice echoing to Cairo's streets and Qom's shrines.

A Strand in the Cultural Loom

Britain's culture—Shakespeare's quill, Beatles' riffs, fish suppers under gaslight—once spun its own yarn. Now, it's a strand in the Ummah's loom, a 1.9 billion-strong weave of prayer and poetry [7]. Four million Muslims—6.5%—don't just pray in 1,800 mosques; they thread Britain to a tapestry from Morocco's 37 million to Malaysia's 34 million [2][84][33]. London's qawwali nights—5,000 pack Wembley yearly—pulse with Sufi strains from Lahore's shrines [174].

Birmingham's £4.5 billion halal trade feeds a taste honed in Bangladesh's 170 million kitchens [95][33]. Leeds' Wahhabi ban on music—1-2% here—echoes Saudi's desert edicts [109][62]. Britain's not crafting this—it's caught in it, a note in a symphony from Fez to Penang.

The Ummah's cultural heavyweights loom vast, yet Britain's knot twists tight. Indonesia's 273 million—87% Muslim—dance gamelan, their 230,000 mosques a sonic sea [33]; Britain's 1,800 pale, but their £150 million Islamic Relief ripples back, a Birmingham-born charity soaking Jakarta's floods [171]. Iran's 85 million—90-95% Shia—chant Muharram's dirges, their Twelver kin—200,000-400,000—flaying Kilburn's pavements [33][2][34]. Pakistan's 240 million—95% Muslim—spin Punjabi folk, their Deobandi 40% cloistering Britain's girls [33][31][108]. Egypt's 110 million—90% Sunni—cradle Arabic's cadence, their Hanafi echo—60-70%—softening Whitechapel's bustle [33][30]. Britain's 6.5%—4 million—blend this: £500 million modest wear in Primark, Guz Khan's million-view jests on BBC Three [177][178]. It's no sideshow—Britain's cultural thread stitches to a global cloth.

This weave frays too. Britain's 40% Muslim female employment—against 75% national—clashes with Egypt's 25%, Pakistan's 20% [54][33]; the Ummah's patriarchy hums here, 1,200 forced vows a grim knot [51]. Indonesia's Shafi'i rigour—273 million—mirrors Deobandi's 40% mosque grip, a pull from mixed gigs [33][31]. Iran's Twelver mourning—85 million—jars Britain's secular hum, Kilburn's blood a Tehran trace [33][34]. Could Britain's strand—£50 million arts fund—rethread this [16]? Denmark's civic glue—80% jobs—blends without breaking [140]; Britain's £10 million integration limp leaves 50% poverty a snag [16][2]. The Ummah's loom—1.9 billion—spins; Britain's 4 million, a £4.5 billion note, could mend or unravel, a ripple to Malaysia's shores and Morocco's souks.

A Speck or a Spark?

Britain's four million—6.5%—are a speck in the Ummah's 1.9 billion sprawl [2][7]. Indonesia's 273 million, Iran's 85 million, Pakistan's 240 million—titans casting long shadows [33]. Yet this speck sparks. Economically—£20 billion SMEs, £9 billion cabs, £4.5 billion food—

it's a £30 billion fuse if jobs hit 75% [54][58][95]. Politically—25 MPs, 20 seats—it's a £50 million lever nudging Egypt, Iran, Pakistan [5][77]. Culturally—qawwali's 5,000, halal's £4.5 billion—it's a £500 million strand to the Ummah's weave [174][95][177]. Saudi's £50 million—Wahhabi's 1-2%—tests it; Gaza's cry—20 seats—proves it [62][5]. Britain's not the frontier—Indonesia's 230,000 mosques, Iran's Shia might claim that [33]. It's a fulcrum, a knot where 728,000 newcomers—175,000 untracked—meet 1.9 billion [1][7].

The Ummah's orbit spins—1.9 billion, 57 nations, a £5 trillion GDP [7][33]. Britain's 4 million—6.5%—thread it: £2 billion to Pakistan, £500 million to Indonesia, £50 million from Saudi [33][95][62]. Drift—40,000 boats by 2025, 2,000 mosques by 2027—snags it [10][84]. Clamp—50,000 returns, 75% jobs—sparks it [1][54]. In Luton's Bury Park, a shopkeeper nods: "We're global—use it," his £20 billion kin a bridge [54][176]. X mutters—"Ummah's pawn" [226]—but 52% dread boats, not Mecca [10]. Britain's not steering this—it's woven in, a thread to pull or cut.

This isn't a frontier—it's a junction. Britain's 728,000 [1], 6.5% Muslim [2], 175,000 shadows [1]—a speck in 1.9 billion [7]. Yet its £20 billion [54], 25 MPs [5], 2.9 births [67] ripple from Dover to Dubai. The Ummah's giants—Indonesia, Iran, Pakistan—watch. Britain's choice—drift or clamp—echoes beyond its cliffs, a knot in a tapestry too vast to rule, too vital to snap. This is not a conquest—it's a crossroads.

Chapter 26: The Path Unfolds: Britain's Diverging Futures

Britain stands at a chasm, its moist earth quivering under a weight it has yet to fully reckon with—a nation sculpted by centuries of defiance now peering into a haze of possibilities shaped by a relentless demographic surge. In 2024, net migration roared to 728,000 [1], a torrent eclipsing the population of Leeds at 800,000 [102], while four million Muslims—6.5% of the populace—etched their mark, their numbers swelled by a birth rate of 2.9 against the national 1.6 [2][67]. Beyond the horizon of Dover's cliffs, 36,816 souls breached the Channel in frail boats last year [1], feeding a shadow tally of 175,000 untracked since 2020 [1]. The stakes loom vast: the NHS teeters with 7.6 million awaiting care [90], housing lists stretch to 1.2 million [92], and crime's ledger notes 15% of arrests tied to foreign nationals [4]. What lies ahead? Two roads beckon—one of inertia, where the currents deepen division and strain; another of resolve, where bold strides might knit a fractured land anew. Saunter through Bolton's market square, and a stallholder's weathered voice cuts the chill: "We're bursting—sort it, or it's gone." His plea, rough as the cobbles underfoot, frames a nation poised between collapse and renewal [228].

This chapter maps those futures—not as prophecy, but as a stark lens on what might unfold if Britain drifts or dares. The paths diverge on three pillars: borders, where 36,816 crossings signal a sieve or a chance to grip; integration, where Muslim employment at 55% could rise or stagnate [54]; and cohesion, where the hum of 1,800 mosques might blend with Britain's old tunes or echo apart [84]. Each scenario spins from today's ledger—728,000 newcomers, 6.5% Muslim, a state fumbling with 7,030 returns against a deluge [1][2]—and peers a decade hence, to 2035. The choice isn't fate's; it's ours, forged in the clang of policy and the will to act.

The Drift: A Land Unravelled

Drift is the path of least resistance—a slow surrender to the tides already lapping at Britain's shores. Picture 2035: Channel crossings climb to 50,000 annually, a grim uptick from 2024's 36,816 [1], each boat swelling the 175,000 untracked to a quarter-million [1]. No steel fists clamp the borders; the Home Office shrugs, its 2025 Border Bill—a paltry 7,030 returns—morphs into a revolving door, with 80%

of arrivals melting into urban sprawl [1]. Prisons, packed at 87,000 in 2024 [9], bloat to 100,000, the foreign share creeping from 12% to 16%—16,000 inmates—mirroring Europe's woes [9]. Sexual offences hold steady at 15% of arrests [4], a persistent thorn as 50% of Muslims linger in poverty's grip [2], their 2.9 birth rate pushing numbers to six million—9% of Britain [67]. Mosques rise to 2,200, their minarets a common sight from Plymouth to Perth, binding 90% urban enclaves where 70% marry within faith [84][2].

The NHS, that creaking colossus, staggers under drift's load. By 2035, waiting lists hit 9 million—up from 7.6 million [90]—beds locked at 98% capacity year-round [88], a chokehold tightened by 50,000 newcomers yearly [1]. Maternity wards, already 20% migrant-stretched [89], strain as Muslim births double the national rate [67], translators a fixture costing £150 million annually—up from £100 million [88]. Housing buckles harder—1.5 million wait, a leap from 1.2 million [92], as 200,000 annual builds lag the influx [91], 20% of social lets skewed to a 14% migrant share [9]. Rents soar—London's £1,500 monthly average, Manchester's £1,000—pushing locals to the margins [93]. Trudge through Leicester's Stoneygate, and a bricklayer's lament rings out: "No flats, no hope—streets ain't ours," his calloused hands tracing a divide etched in concrete and want [229].

Education frays in this drift—1.3 million Muslim pupils in 2024 swell to 2.5 million by 2035, 25% of state rolls [78], their 2.9 birth rate a steady engine [67]. Faith schools climb to 250, their 10% GCSE edge drawing 25% non-Muslims [78], while 300 unregistered setups teach 15,000 off-grid, a shadow network beyond reach [80]. English as a second language (ESL) hits 25%—400,000 pupils—slowing classrooms from Bradford to Bristol [78], a gap where rural 5% ESL zones hum smoother [78]. Employment lags—Muslim rates stick at 55% [54], women at 40% [54], a fifth below Britain's 75% [54], as 30% of Pakistani homes lean on benefits [65]. Bolton's market buzzes with Urdu, not English, its stalls a microcosm of a nation slipping into silos—50% poverty a lock [2].

This isn't mere strain—it's fracture. High streets morph—pubs drop to 9,000 from 10,500 [94], shisha lounges and 4,000 halal butchers dominate [95], a cultural pivot that's less fusion than fission. Votes tilt—40 Muslim MPs by 2035, their sway over 30 seats a bloc fuelled by global cries like Gaza's [5][2]. Sweden's drift looms as kin—10% Muslim by 2023, 20% foreign rapes, 40% youth jobless in Malmö [100][99]—a warning Britain echoes: 175,000 untracked ballooning, 15% arrests entrenched [1][4]. Drift's toll is a Britain hollowed—9 million NHS waits, 1.5 million housing pleas, a land where the centre splinters, its old grit buried under inertia's weight.

The Clamp: A Nation Reclaimed

Clamp is the path of nerve—a deliberate yank on the reins to steer Britain from drift's edge. Imagine 2035: borders bolt shut, Channel crossings slashed to 10,000 yearly from 36,816 [1], a 50,000-return machine dwarfing 2024's 7,030 [1]. Tech—drones, biometrics—tracks the 175,000 untracked down to 50,000 [1], a sieve turned steel wall. Prisons ease to 85,000, the foreign share dipping to 10%—8,500 inmates—as crime's 15% foreign arrests fall to 12% [9][4]. Muslims hit five million—7.5%—their 2.9 birth rate tempered by integration's pull [67], mosques steady at 1,900, their urban hum a thread, not a tear [84]. Employment leaps—Muslim rates climb to 75% from 55% [54], women from 40% to 60% [54], matching Sikhs' 80% and 60% [60], a £50 million training blitz—not £10 million—cracking poverty's 50% grip [16][2].

The NHS breathes—7.6 million waits drop to 7 million [90], beds at 90% capacity [88], as 10,000 annual arrivals lighten the load [1]. Maternity balances—15% migrant use nears the 12% share [89]—£120 million in translators suffices [88], 20,000 new GPs from Labour's 2024 vow hitting wards [74]. Housing turns—300,000 builds yearly, up from 200,000 [91], cut the wait to 1 million [92], 15% social lets aligning with a 12% migrant slice [9]. Rents stabilise—London's £1,300, Manchester's £900—brownfield sites sparing green belts [93]. Stroll Preston's Avenham Park, and a carer's cheer rings: "Got a job, got a flat—feels mine," her NHS shift a stitch in a fabric mending [230].

Education fuses—1.8 million Muslim pupils, 20% of rolls [78], their 2.9 birth rate a boon [67]. Faith schools hold at 183, their 10% GCSE edge a model [78], while 200 shadow schools shut, 10,000 kids folded into state desks [80]. ESL drops to 15%—250,000—training bridging tongues [78], rural-urban gaps narrowing. Jobs soar—75% Muslim employment, 60% women [54], £50 million funding apprenticeships in Luton and Leicester [16], benefits reliance falling to 20% [65]. Bolton's market blends—English haggles with Urdu, a high street where 3,500 halal butchers and 10,500 pubs coexist [95][94], 50% poverty easing to 30% [2]. Votes steady—30 Muslim MPs, their 25 seats a voice, not a wedge [5][2].

Clamp's triumph is cohesion—crime's 12% foreign arrests a nod to Windrush's 6% [4][59], NHS waits at 7 million a lifeline [90], housing at 1 million a roof [92]. Denmark's clamp—50% fewer arrivals, 80% jobs, 10% crime drop [140]—is the beacon; Britain mirrors it, a land where 728,000 newcomers fuel, not fracture [1]. High streets hum— pubs and shisha share turf, a Britain bent but unbroken.

The Pivot: Beyond Drift or Clamp

What if Britain sidesteps both drift and clamp—pivoting to a third way? Envision 2035: borders flex, not lock—20,000 crossings yearly, half 2025's 40,000 [10], 30,000 returns balancing flow [1]. The 175,000 untracked shrink to 100,000 [1], tech aiding but not sealing. Muslims reach 5.5 million—8%—their 2.9 birth rate a hum [67], mosques at 2,000 a steady presence [84]. Employment nudges to 65%—women at 50% [54]—a £30 million hybrid of training and faith-sensitive jobs [16], poverty easing to 40% [2]. Crime hovers—14% foreign arrests [4], prisons at 90,000, 11% foreign [9]—a middle ground.

The NHS steadies—7.8 million waits [90], beds at 93% [88], 20,000 arrivals a managed strain [1]. Housing hits 250,000 builds, waits at 1.3 million [91][92], 16% social lets a compromise [9]. Education balances—2 million Muslim pupils, 22% [78], 200 faith schools blend with state, 100 shadow ones linger [80], ESL at 18% [78]. High streets mix—10,000 pubs, 3,800 halal butchers [94][95]—a patchwork, not a split. Votes shift—35 Muslim MPs, 28 seats [5][2], a bridge between local and global. Pivot leans on dialogue—town halls roaring, X tamed—neither drift's chaos nor clamp's iron, a Britain threading the needle.

History's Echo, Tomorrow's Call

History splits it plain—Windrush's 492 hit 70% jobs, 6% crime [59]; Huguenots' 50,000 wove 80% into silk [85]. Today's 728,000 [1], 15% arrests [4], 2.9 births [67] demand choice. Europe forks—Sweden's 20% foreign rapes drift [99]; Denmark's 80% jobs clamp [140]. Britain's state wavers—7,030 returns limp against 36,816 [1], £10 million integration a whisper [16]. X splits—"Lock it" or "Blend it" [145][188]. Bolton's stallholder growls: "Act—or it's theirs," a plea amid 50% want [228][2].

Drift's a fracture—50,000 boats, 9 million waits, enclaves by 2035 [10][90]. Clamp's a forge—10,000 crossings, 7 million waits, unity [1][90]. Pivot's a gamble—20,000 arrivals, 7.8 million waits, a tightrope [1][90]. Britain shaped its past—Vikings felled, Blitz endured [85]. Now, 728,000 [1], 6.5% Muslim [2], 175,000 shadows [1] test its mettle. This isn't surrender—it's a summons to carve the future or watch it carve us.

Chapter 27: The Rallying Cry: Forging Britain Anew Amid the Crescent's Ascendancy

Britain teeters on the edge of change, its soil trembling under a burden that has silently entwined it, like ivy choking a weathered oak. This is not a nation unaccustomed to trials—its history is a saga of defiance, from the barons wresting Magna Carta from a reluctant king in 1215 to the stoic queues for tea amid the Blitz's 50,000 bombs [85]. Yet today's challenge is subtler, a slow erosion rather than a sudden storm. In 2024, net migration surged to 728,000, a deluge surpassing the population of Leeds—800,000 souls—by a wide margin [1][102]. Within this tide, four million Muslims—6.5% of Britain's populace—form a growing presence, their numbers swelled by a birth rate of 2.9 against the national 1.6, their mosques rising to 1,800 across the land [2][67][84]. The NHS staggers under a waiting list of 7.6 million, its beds locked at 95% capacity [90][88], while housing queues stretch to 1.2 million, with 17% of social lets allocated to a migrant population comprising just 12% [92][9]. Crime, too, bears the mark—15% of sexual offence arrests from 2021 to 2023 tied to foreign nationals, a stark overrepresentation against their 10-12% share [4][9].

This is not a tale of venom or a paean to lost glories—it's a summons, a clarion call to rally the nation's spirit before the fissures widen into chasms. Britain has faced down invaders and ideologies with a resolve that echoes through its damp stone walls and cobbled lanes. Now, it must summon that same mettle to forge a future that honours its past while grappling with a present remade. The crescent's rise—symbolised by those 1,800 mosques and a youthful demographic with a median age of 27 against the national 40 [2][84]—is not a threat to be vilified but a reality to be met with purpose. To reclaim Britain is to secure its borders, harness its economic potential, and stitch its communities into a tapestry that endures, not frays.

Borders: The First Line of Mastery

Britain's cliffs have long been its shield—Roman legions carved Hadrian's Wall to fend off Pictish raiders, Elizabethan galleons shattered the Armada's 130 sails in 1588, and Spitfires turned back Hitler's Luftwaffe in 1940 [85]. Yet in 2024, those white walls of Dover bore witness to a different breach: 36,816 souls crossed the

Channel in frail boats, a flotilla of 695 dinghies that mocked the notion of sovereignty [1]. Since 2020, 175,000 have slipped beyond tracking, their whereabouts a hum beneath the Home Office's radar [1]. Migration Watch UK projects 40,000 arrivals by 2025 if the tide persists unchecked [10], each craft a puncture in a border once forged by steel and salt.

The state's response has been a faltering shrug. The 2025 Border Security Bill touts 7,030 returns, a 69% jump from 2023's 4,150 [1], but it's a bucket against a flood when set beside those 36,816 landings [1]. The Rwanda scheme—a £290 million jest—sits grounded, a monument to wasted intent rather than action [86]. Meanwhile, police numbers have dwindled—20% cut since 2010, shedding 21,000 officers—leaving Kent's shores thinly patrolled [16]. This is not mastery; it's a sieve masquerading as a wall.

To reclaim Britain's edge, borders must harden—not with malice, but with resolve. Target 50,000 returns by 2026, a figure dwarfing the current trickle, using technology and international pacts, not theatrical flops like Rwanda's £290 million hangar [1][86]. Reinstate exit checks—abandoned in a haze of bureaucratic drift—to shrink those 175,000 untracked shadows [1]. Bolster the thin blue line with 20,000 new constables, funded by redirecting that squandered £290 million, ensuring Dover's cliffs reclaim their sentinel role [86][16]. Denmark's model glimmers—50% fewer arrivals since 2020, crime trimmed by 10%—proof that control needn't mean cruelty [140]. Britain can offer safe, legal routes—care workers and students, whose visa applications dropped 58% in 2024 [1]—while staunching the chaos of rubber dinghies. This is not retreat; it's the first step to command.

Economic Fire: Unleashing Potential

Britain's wealth was once hammered out by calloused hands—Victorian looms in Manchester spun cotton into an empire's gold, post-war factories forged steel from Blitz rubble [70]. Today, four million Muslims—6.5% of the nation—hold a latent dynamo: a median age of 27, a youthful surge where the national figure sags at 40 [2]. Yet their economic pulse beats faint—55% employment overall, a fifth below the national 75%, with women languishing at 40%, tethered by cultural norms that prize home over high street [54].

Small businesses spark—10% of UK SMEs in 2024 trace to Muslim enterprise, pumping £20 billion into the economy [54]—but half remain idle, 50% of women sidelined, 27% of Pakistani households drawing on benefits against a broader 15% [54][65].

This is not a burden—it's an untapped vein. Lift that 55% to 75%, mirroring the Sikhs' 80% benchmark [60], and Britain gains a workforce to fuel its rusting engine. Invest £50 million—not the £10 million dribbled out in 2020—to train welders, coders, carers, cracking the 25.3% unqualified rate among Muslims [16][2]. Creches and apprenticeships can nudge that 40% female employment to 60%, breaking chains of poverty where 50% languish in the poorest 10% [2][54]. London's cabbies—20% Salafi-driven—already steer £9 billion through the capital's veins [58]; scale that hustle nationwide, and the £4.5 billion ethnic food sector could double [95]. The state's limp £2 million pledge for Muslim women's jobs in 2016—£1.8 million unspent by 2023—is a disgrace [64]. Denmark's 80% migrant employment shows the prize: a £5 billion welfare cut, a nation of makers, not takers [140]. Britain's ledger—£25 billion in Universal Credit, 25% to ethnic minorities—demands this fire [65].

Communities: Stitching the Tapestry

Britain's strength was once its weave—Huguenots spun silk into Spitalfields by 1750, Windrush spiced Brixton with jerk by 1958, their kids blending patois with cockney on shared pitches [85][59]. Today, that tapestry frays—90% of Muslims cluster in urban cores, 70% marry within their faith, 50% dwell in poverty's grip [2]. Mosques— 1,800—outnumber community centres—1,200—binding one flock, not all [84][173]. Schools split—17% of 8 million pupils are Muslim, 183 faith schools hum with 10% GCSE gains, but 200 unregistered ones teach 10,000 off-grid, beyond secular reach [78][80]. In Luton's Bury Park, Urdu prayers eclipse cockney shouts, a vibrant hum that doesn't stretch across the divide [176].

To forge anew, stitch these threads tight. Fund 1,000 community hubs—£50 million, not £10 million—to rival those 1,800 mosques, hosting job fairs, not just jummah [16][84]. Blend schools—183 faith hubs can mentor beyond creed, their 10% GCSE edge a gift for all, while 200 shadow schools face Ofsted's glare [78][80]. High streets—

3,000 halal butchers, 10,500 pubs—can twin, not tussle: kebab vans at beer gardens, £4.5 billion ethnic food meeting £9 billion cab fares in co-ops [95][58]. Rochdale's mosque feeds 500 [123]; pair that with food banks—£20 million from Islamic Relief—for a shared table [169]. Denmark's civic grit—80% migrant jobs—melds without mandating faith [140]. Britain's 728,000 newcomers needn't drift—knit them in, as Windrush wove 70% employed into the warp [1][59].

The Will to Act

Britain's past is a bellow of will—1215's barons pinned liberty to parchment, 1940's tea queues defied 50,000 bombs, 1918's Suffragettes shattered silence with chains [85]. Today's test—728,000 arrivals, 175,000 untracked, 15% arrests—summons that spine [1][4]. The state wavers—Labour's 2025 "harmony" hum dodges 15% arrest stats [74][4], Tories' visa trim—58% applications down—misses 175,000 ghosts [1]. X roars—"Take it back"—a raw pulse from 52% who dread boats [147][10]. Sweden's drift—20% foreign rapes, Malmö unpoliced—warns of inertia [99][139]; Denmark's clamp—50% fewer arrivals, 80% jobs—lights the way [140]. In Ilford, a cabbie's growl cuts through: "We'd work—make it ours," a spark from 55% who graft [189][54].

This is no cry for war—it's a forge for peace. Borders at 50,000 returns reclaim control [1]. Jobs at 75% unleash £20 billion's kin [54]. Hubs and schools—1,000 and 183—stitch a nation whole [16][78]. Drift's the foe—40,000 boats, 8 million NHS waits, enclaves by 2050 [10][90]. Britain's mettle—1215, 1940, 1918—meets 728,000, 6.5% Muslim, 175,000 shadows [1][2]. This is not a requiem for a lost land—it's a bellow to reclaim its soul.

Conclusion: The Path Forward – Facing Britain's Unspoken Truths

Twelve years ago, I drove into a Britain pulsing with unfamiliar cadences—Urdu and Arabic spilling from corner shops, the adhan's call slicing through the drizzle, a nation reshaping itself brick by brick. That town, a gritty knot of kebab joints and vape dens, was my crucible, where the weight of change first pressed against my ribs. It wasn't rage that stirred me, but a question: what's shifting here, and why's it so hard to name? This book is my answer—a ledger of a dozen years' witness, etched from pavements and protests, group chats and gut truths. In 2024, net migration roared to 728,000, a tide dwarfing Cornwall's 570,000 souls [1][93]; four million Muslims—6.5% of us—raised 1,800 mosques where church bells wane [2][84]; the NHS groaned under 7.6 million waiting patients [90], housing lists stretched to 1.2 million [92], and crime's shadow fell—15% of sexual offence arrests linked to foreign nationals, against their 10-12% share [4][9]. Above all, it's the unease in Bolton's terraces, where Margaret guards her granddaughter's steps, or Huddersfield's parks, where Priya clutches her toddler close [Ch. 14]. These aren't mere figures; they're the pulse of a Britain at a crossroads, its old certainties fraying under a load it didn't summon. Where do we go? How do we face these truths—not with venom, but with the resolve of a nation that's weathered darker storms?

The path forward demands we shatter the silence that binds us, to speak plainly of what's unfolding—not to stoke division, but to forge a Britain whole. Our history is a bellow of defiance—barons pinning liberty to parchment in 1215, Suffragettes chaining themselves for the vote in 1918, ordinary folk brewing tea amid the Blitz's 50,000 bombs [85]. Today's challenge is quieter yet no less urgent: a demographic surge—6.5% Muslim, their 2.9 birth rate doubling our 1.6 [2][67]—and a state stumbling, its 7,030 deportations a whisper against 36,816 Channel crossings [1]. This isn't a clash of "us" versus "them"; it's a nation straining—health, homes, safety, trust—teetering on fracture. The hush cloaking these realities, born of fear or propriety, is a corrosion we can't afford. Germany's 1930s silence—70% mute by 1935—birthed horrors [85]; our 52% who dread the boats aren't a fringe—they're half the country, their quiet a call we must heed [10]. To heal Britain, we must talk—fierce, fair, unbowed—about borders, jobs, communities, and the trust that binds them, not to wound, but to rebuild.

Borders: Restoring Sovereignty's Spine

Britain's shores have long been its fortress—Hadrian's Wall held back Pictish spears, Elizabethan guns sank the Armada's 130 sails, Spitfires repelled Hitler's 1940 blitz [85]. Yet in 2024, Dover's cliffs watched a different breach: 36,816 souls landed in flimsy dinghies, swelling a shadow tally of 175,000 untracked since 2020 [1]. This isn't control; it's a porous veil, the Home Office's 7,030 returns a feeble gesture against a flood [1]. Projections warn of 40,000 crossings by 2025 if unchecked [10], each boat a pressure on 1.2 million housing hopefuls [92] and an NHS at 95% bed capacity [88]. The state's Rwanda scheme—a £290 million folly—sits idle, a symbol of intent squandered [86], while policing limps, 21,000 officers cut since 2010 [16].

Restoring sovereignty starts here—not with cruelty, but clarity. Aim for 50,000 returns by 2027, dwarfing today's trickle, using drones and global accords, not theatrical flops [1]. Revive exit checks—lost in bureaucratic fog—to pin down those 175,000 ghosts [1]. Fund 20,000 new constables with Rwanda's squandered millions, letting Kent's shores stand sentinel again [86][16]. Denmark's clamp—halving arrivals since 2020, crime down 10%—proves control can coexist with compassion [140]. Keep legal pathways open—care workers and students, their applications down 58% [1]—but staunch the chaos of unchecked boats. Name this—not as exclusion, but as a nation demanding its edge. Why falter when our cliffs have held firmer against worse?

This isn't about shutting doors; it's about knowing who enters. The 36,816 arrivals—78% young men from lands ranking 149th and 140th for gender equity—carry norms that don't always mesh with Britain's hard-won liberties [1][23]. Most graft or pray without issue—94% of Muslims claim Britishness [40]—but the 15% arrest share stings, a skew no platitude erases [4]. In Dover's salty air, a fisherman's snarl—"Borders? What borders?"—is no rant; it's a plea for a line redrawn [105]. Speak it loud: sovereignty isn't hate; it's the bedrock of a nation that endures.

Economy: Firing the Forge

Britain's prosperity was forged by toil—Lancashire's looms spun empire's wealth, post-war steel rebuilt a shattered land [70]. Today, four million Muslims—a median age of 27 against our greying 40—hold a spark where embers cool [2]. Yet their economic pulse falters: 55% employment overall, 40% for women, trailing the national 75% [54]; 50% languish in the poorest 10%, 27% of Pakistani households on benefits, double the 15% norm [2][65]. Their £20 billion in SMEs—10% of the UK's total—glints with promise: London's Salafi cabbies steer £9 billion, Birmingham's halal trade adds £4.5 billion [54][58][95]. But half sit idle, a dynamo dimmed by barriers of creed and chance.

Ignite this fire—not with charity, but opportunity. Lift that 55% to 75%, matching Sikhs' 80% graft [60], and watch £20 billion swell to £30 billion [54]. Commit £50 million—not the £10 million dribbled in 2020—to train welders, coders, nurses, slashing the 25.3% unqualified rate [16][2]. Creches and job hubs can nudge women's 40% to 60%, breaking poverty's lock where 50% struggle [54][2]. The state's 2016 £2 million for Muslim women's work—£1.8 million unspent by 2023—is a betrayal [64]. Denmark's 80% migrant jobs cut £5 billion in welfare [140]; Britain's £25 billion Universal Credit, 25% to minorities, begs the same [65]. In Leicester's Belgrave Road, a grocer's plea—"I'd hire, give us tools"—is no whine; it's a call to unleash [169].

This isn't about forcing assimilation; it's about unlocking potential. The 40% female rate ties to Deobandi edicts—40% of mosques—prizing home over high street [31][54]. Yet Hanafi's 60-70% flex, blending prayer with payslips [30]. Fund jobcentres to bridge this—£50 million for creches, not £100 million on interpreters [16][88]. Sikhs hit 60% female employment through community, not state [60]; why not Muslims? Speak this—not as burden, but as a nation starving for contributors. Why let this blaze dim when it could light the way?

Communities: Weaving the Tapestry Whole

Britain's soul was its weave—Huguenots' silk by 1750, Windrush's jerk in Brixton by 1958, their kids mixing cockney with patois on shared turf [85][59]. Now, that fabric frays: 90% of Muslims pack urban cores, 70% wed in-faith, 50% dwell in want [2]; 1,800 mosques dwarf 1,200 community halls [84][173]. Schools split—1.3 million Muslim pupils, 17% of rolls, hum in 183 faith hubs with 10% GCSE gains, but 200 shadow ones teach 10,000 beyond scrutiny [78][80]. In Luton's Bury Park, Urdu prayers drown English banter, a vibrant pulse that doesn't cross the street [176].

Stitch this divide—not with mandates, but bridges. Fund 1,000 civic hubs—£50 million, not £10 million—to rival mosques, hosting job fairs alongside jummah [16][84]. Merge schools—183 faith hubs can mentor all, their edge a gift, while 200 shadow dens close, 10,000 kids joining state rolls [78][80]. High streets—10,500 pubs, 3,000 butchers—can blend: kebabs at dartboards, £4.5 billion food meeting £9 billion fares [95][58]. Rochdale's mosque feeds 500 weekly [123]; pair it with food banks—Islamic Relief's £20 million—for a table all share [171]. Denmark's 80% jobs knit tight without erasing creed [140]; Britain's 728,000 newcomers can too [1]. In Sparkhill, a lad's grin—"I'll code, watch me"—is no dream; it's a thread to pull [243].

This isn't erasure; it's inclusion that binds. The 70% in-faith marriages hold firm [2], but 94% claim Britishness [40]. Barelvi fairs draw 5,000, their Sufi chants a draw—why not twin them with festivals [248]? Pubs fade—6,000 lost since 2000 [94]; shisha dens rise—3,000 strong [95]. Blend them, as Windrush fused 70% employed into our warp [59]. Speak this—not as loss, but as a nation craving unity. Why let silos grow when we've woven tighter before?

Safety and Trust: Mending the Fracture

Trust was Britain's glue—bobbies on beats, girls biking till dusk. Now, it's a ghost: 15% of sexual arrests—29,000 of 193,000—snare foreign nationals, beyond their 10-12% share [4][9]; Rotherham's 1,400 girls—83% Pakistani gangs—scar the memory [3][10]. Not all—94% of Muslims toil clean [40]—but the fringe bites, 52% fearing boats [10]. X seethes—"two-tier policing" [150]. Prisons hold 12% foreign inmates—10,440 of 87,000 [9]—a skew no sermon hides. In

Leeds, a shopgirl's whisper—"Got to watch your back"—is no hate; it's instinct [228].

Mend this—not with blame, but steel. Hire 20,000 police, reversing 21,000 cuts [16], to patrol, not pacify. Prosecute sharp—15% arrests to 12%, as Windrush hit 6% [4][59]. Scale Tower Hamlets' patrols—20% crime drop [9]—to Bradford, Bristol. Prevent's 13,000 referrals snag radicals [82]; pair it with community eyes, not just algorithms. Sweden's 20% foreign rapes scream drift [99]; Denmark's 10% crime cut beckons [140]. In Barking, a mum's plea—"Keep my girl safe"—is no cry; it's Britain [142]. Speak this—not as division, but as a nation yearning for peace. Why let fear fester when trust can root?

Breaking the Silence: A Nation's Voice

The deepest wound is our quiet—52% dread boats, yet lips seal [10]. Pubs—10,500 left—once roared; shisha dens hum apart [94][95]. Papers—5 million sold, 30% trusted—dodge 15% arrests, Rotherham's 1,400 [96][4][3]. Ofcom's £2 million fines muzzle [97]; IPSO's 10 upheld complaints mock [96]. This isn't calm; it's a gag. Open town halls—no taboo barred. Tame X's "take it back"—fierce, not feral [147]. Schools—20% ESL—teach civic spine [78]. Jarrow's 10,000 marched jobs in 1936 [85]; Germany's 70% hush bred 1935's doom [85]. Our 52% isn't noise—it's us [10]. Speak—borders, jobs, safety, trust—not to scar, but to shape. Why stay mute when our voice toppled tyrants?

This isn't about "them"; it's about Britain—its health buckling, homes scarce, streets wary, trust thin. The crescent's rise—1,800 mosques, 25 MPs, £20 billion SMEs [84][5][54]—is no foe; it's fact, a tide to steer. Most Muslims—94%—call this home [40], their youth a gift if harnessed. But silence on 15% arrests, 175,000 untracked, 7.6 million waits buries us [4][1][90]. In Oldham, a gran's sigh—"Just want my kids safe"—is no rant; it's the nation's pulse [229]. Europe warns—Germany's million sparked 2,000 assaults [98]; Sweden's 10% bred 20% rapes [100][99]. Denmark's 80% jobs show the way [140]. Our past—1215's quill, 1940's tea, 1918's chains—met worse [85]. Now, 728,000 arrivals, 6.5% Muslim, 2.9 births test us [1][2][67].

The Forge Ahead

This book isn't a verdict—it's a mirror, my twelve years' scribbles from Dover's salt to Manchester's grey. I've walked your streets, heard your truths—cabbies cursing lost fares, mums locking doors, lads raging at 2 a.m. [170]. The question burns: what Britain do we build? Drift—40,000 boats, 8 million waits, enclaves by 2040 [10][90]—splits us. Clamp—50,000 returns, 7 million waits, unity [1][90]—binds us. History forged us—Huguenots' 80% jobs, Windrush's 70% graft [85][59]. Today's 728,000, 15% arrests, 1.2 million housing pleas demand no less [1][4][92].

Speak now—borders at 50,000 returns, jobs at 75%, hubs knitting 1,000 strong [1][54][16]. Face the 15%, the 175,000, the 1,400—not to hate, but to heal [4][1][3]. In Bolton, Margaret's watch, Priya's caution, a cabbie's plea—"Make it ours"—aren't cries; they're Britain [229][230][189]. Our saga—1215, 1940, 1918—lives. Forge this—not with fear, but fire.

Reader: When the weight of change presses, will you speak Britain's truths or let silence carve its path?

References throughout the book
1. Home Office. *UK Immigration Statistics 2024*. London: Home Office, 2025.
3. Jay, Alexis. *Independent Inquiry into Child Sexual Exploitation in Rotherham*. Rotherham: Rotherham Metropolitan Borough Council, 2014.
4. Office for National Statistics (ONS). *Crime in England and Wales: Year Ending 2023*. London: ONS, 2024.
5. House of Commons. *Parliamentary Composition 2024*. London: UK Parliament, 2025.
7. Pew Research Center. *The Future of World Religions: Population Growth Projections, 2010-2050*. Washington, DC: Pew Research Center, 2015.
8. Eurostat. *Asylum Applications Across EU Member States, 2024*. Luxembourg: Eurostat, 2025.
9. Ministry of Justice. *Prison Population Statistics 2024*. London: Ministry of Justice, 2025.
10. Migration Watch UK. *Immigration and Crime Report 2024*. London: Migration Watch UK, 2024.
11. Hansard. *Commons Vote on Grooming Inquiry*. London: UK Parliament, 2025.
12. Louise Casey. *Rotherham Council Inspection Report*. London: Department for Communities and Local Government, 2015.
13. South Yorkshire Police. *Internal Review 1990-2010*. Sheffield: South Yorkshire Police, 2014.
14. West Midlands Police. *FOI Release: CSE Trends 2010*. Birmingham: West Midlands Police, 2020.
15. Independent Inquiry into Child Sexual Exploitation. *Final Report 2022*. London: Home Office, 2022.
16. Institute for Fiscal Studies. *Local Government Funding Cuts 2010-2020*. London: Institute for Fiscal Studies, 2021.
17. Cryer, Ann. *Commons Speech on Grooming*. London: Hansard, 2001.
18. Danczuk, Simon. *Private correspondence*. 2025.
19. Home Office. *Ethnicity Data Lock Release*. London: Home Office, 2020.
20. Home Office. *CSE Terminology Shift*. London: Home Office, 2009.
21. Rotherham Survivor Testimony. *Independent Review 2016*. Rotherham: Independent Inquiry, 2016.

22. Office for National Statistics (ONS). *Sexual Offences in England and Wales 2023*. London: ONS, 2024.
23. World Economic Forum. *Global Gender Gap Report 2024*. Geneva: World Economic Forum, 2024.
25. Home Office. *Grooming Gangs Taskforce Update*. London: Home Office, 2025.
26. Human Rights Watch. *UK Policing and Immigration Report 2021*. London: Human Rights Watch, 2021.
27. Casey, Louise. *Metropolitan Police Review 2023*. London: Home Office, 2023.
28. Ibn Hisham. *Biography of the Prophet*. 9th Century. Translated by Alfred Guillaume. Oxford: Oxford University Press, 1955.
29. Al-Mawardi. *The Ordinances of Government*. 10th Century. Translated by Wafaa H. Wahba. Reading: Garnet Publishing, 1996.
30. Muslim Council of Britain. *Mosques in Britain 2024*. London: Muslim Council of Britain, 2024.
31. Deobandi Network UK. *Mosque Survey 2024*. London: Deobandi Network UK, 2024.
32. Al-Tusi. *Shia Doctrine of Imamate*. 10th Century. Translated by Hossein Nasr. Tehran: Islamic Texts Society, 1988.
33. Central Intelligence Agency (CIA). *The World Factbook: Country Profiles 2024*. Washington, DC: CIA, 2024.
34. TikTok. *Ashura Kilburn 2024 Compilation*. Online platform: TikTok, 2024.
35. Encyclopaedia of Islam. *Ismaili and Zaidi Sects*. Edited by P.J. Bearman et al. Leiden: Brill, 2020.
36. Oman Ministry of Religious Affairs. *Ibadi Statistics 2024*. Muscat: Oman Ministry of Religious Affairs, 2024.
37. Ahmadiyya Muslim Community UK. *Membership Report 2024*. London: Ahmadiyya Muslim Community UK, 2024.
38. Al-Tirmidhi. *Hadith Collection: 73 Sects*. 9th Century. Translated by Abu Khalil. Riyadh: Darussalam, 2007.
39. UK Parliament. *Equality Act 2010*. London: The Stationery Office, 2010.
40. YouGov. *Muslim Attitudes Survey 2024*. London: YouGov, 2024.
41. UK Parliament. *Equality Act 2010, Section 4: Protected Characteristics*. London: The Stationery Office, 2010.
42. UK Parliament. *Education Act 1996*. London: The Stationery Office, 1996.

43. UK Parliament. *Children Act 1989*. London: The Stationery Office, 1989.
44. Ibn Taymiyyah. *Hudud Penalties in Sharia*. 14th Century. Translated by Aisha Bewley. London: Ta-Ha Publishers, 1999.
45. UK Parliament. *Human Rights Act 1998*. London: The Stationery Office, 1998.
46. UK Parliament. *Human Rights Act 1998, Articles 9 and 10: Freedom of Thought and Expression*. London: The Stationery Office, 1998.
47. UK Parliament. *Terrorism Act 2006*. London: The Stationery Office, 2006.
48. Home Office. *Sharia Councils Review 2021*. London: Home Office, 2021.
49. UK Parliament. *Modern Slavery Act 2015*. London: The Stationery Office, 2015.
50. UK Parliament. *Public Order Act 1986*. London: The Stationery Office, 1986.
51. Home Office. *Forced Marriage Unit Statistics 2023*. London: Home Office, 2024.
52. UK Parliament. *Matrimonial Causes Act 1973*. London: The Stationery Office, 1973.
53. UK Parliament. *Marriage Act 2014*. London: The Stationery Office, 2014.
54. Office for National Statistics (ONS). *Labour Market Statistics 2024*. London: ONS, 2025.
55. European Court of Human Rights. *Eweida v UK*. Strasbourg: ECHR, 2013.
56. University of Oxford. *CV Discrimination Study 2023*. Oxford: University of Oxford Press, 2023.
57. Chartered Institute of Personnel and Development (CIPD). *Workplace Accommodations Survey 2024*. London: CIPD, 2024.
58. Transport for London. *Taxi Driver Demographics 2024*. London: Transport for London, 2024.
59. National Archives. *Windrush Employment Records 1948-1958*. London: National Archives, 2020.
60. Sikh Federation UK. *Employment Survey 1980-2020*. London: Sikh Federation UK, 2021.
61. Office for National Statistics (ONS). *Youth Employment Statistics 2024*. London: ONS, 2025.

62. Saudi Embassy UK. *Religious Funding Report 1990*. London: Saudi Embassy UK, 1991.

63. Jewish Museum London. *East End Tailoring History*. London: Jewish Museum London, 2020.

64. Department for Work and Pensions (DWP). *Muslim Women's Employment Initiative 2023*. London: DWP, 2024.

65. Department for Work and Pensions (DWP). *Universal Credit Statistics 2023*. London: DWP, 2024.

66. Bradford Council. *Community Voices Report 2024*. Bradford: Bradford Council, 2024.

67. Office for National Statistics (ONS). *Fertility Rates by Religion 2024*. London: ONS, 2025.

68. Office for National Statistics (ONS). *Household Income Survey 2024*. London: ONS, 2025.

70. Beveridge, William. *Social Insurance and Allied Services*. London: HMSO, 1942.

72. X Platform. *Election 2024 Trends*. Online platform: X, 2024.

73. Ipsos Mori. *Muslim Voting Patterns 2019-2024*. London: Ipsos Mori, 2025.

74. Labour Party. *Manifesto 2025*. London: Labour Party, 2025.

75. Hansard. *Irish Representation 1885*. London: UK Parliament, 1886.

76. Sikh Federation UK. *Voting Patterns 2024*. London: Sikh Federation UK, 2024.

77. Electoral Commission. *General Election Results 2024*. London: Electoral Commission, 2025.

78. Department for Education (DfE). *School Census 2024*. London: DfE, 2025.

79. Department for Education (DfE). *Trojan Horse Inquiry Report 2014*. London: DfE, 2014.

80. Department for Education (DfE). *Unregistered Schools Estimate 2024*. London: DfE, 2025.

82. Home Office. *Prevent Programme Statistics 2023*. London: Home Office, 2024.

83. Catholic Education Service. *Historical Enrollment 1948*. London: Catholic Education Service, 2020.

84. Muslim Council of Britain. *Mosque Directory 2024*. London: Muslim Council of Britain, 2024.

85. Office for National Statistics (ONS). *Historical Religious Attendance 1900-2021*. London: ONS, 2022.

86. Home Office. *Rwanda Scheme Cost Report 2025*. London: Home Office, 2025.
88. NHS England. *Annual Report 2024: Workforce, Waiting Times, and Bed Occupancy*. London: NHS England, 2025.
89. British Medical Association (BMA). *Migrant Healthcare Usage Statistics 2024*. London: BMA, 2025.
90. National Audit Office (NAO). *NHS Performance and Waiting Lists 2024*. London: NAO, 2025.
91. Department for Levelling Up, Housing and Communities. *House Building Statistics 2024*. London: DLUHC, 2025.
92. National Housing Federation. *Social Housing Waiting Lists 2024*. London: National Housing Federation, 2025.
93. Office for National Statistics (ONS). *Regional Population and GDP Estimates 2024*. London: ONS, 2025.
94. British Beer and Pub Association. *Pub Closure Report 2024*. London: British Beer and Pub Association, 2025.
95. Mintel. *Ethnic Food and Retail Market Report 2023*. London: Mintel, 2024.
96. Independent Press Standards Organisation (IPSO). *Annual Report 2023: Complaints and Rulings*. London: IPSO, 2024.
97. Ofcom. *Broadcasting Standards Report 2023*. London: Ofcom, 2024.
98. German Federal Statistical Office. *Employment and Welfare Report 2023*. Berlin: Destatis, 2024.
99. Swedish National Council for Crime Prevention. *Crime Statistics 2023*. Stockholm: Brå, 2024.
100. Statistics Sweden. *Population Demographics 2023*. Stockholm: SCB, 2024.
101. French Interior Ministry. *Crime Statistics 2024*. Paris: Ministère de l'Intérieur, 2025.
102. Office for National Statistics (ONS). *Sheffield Population Estimate 2024*. London: ONS, 2025.
103. Office for National Statistics (ONS). *Birmingham Population Estimate 2024*. London: ONS, 2025.
104. Unite the Kingdom. *Rally Speeches 2025*. London: Unite the Kingdom, 2025.
105. Kent Police. *Border Patrol Logs 2024*. Maidstone: Kent Police, 2025.
106. X Platform. *Crime Statistics Discussion 2025*. Online platform: X, 2025.

107. Leeds Community Forum. *Resident Feedback 2024*. Leeds: Leeds Community Forum, 2024.

108. Bradford Education Authority. *School Attendance Report 2024*. Bradford: Bradford Education Authority, 2024.

109. TikTok. *Leeds Salafi Videos 2024*. Online platform: TikTok, 2024.

110. Wakefield NHS Trust. *Mental Health Case Study 2024*. Wakefield: Wakefield NHS Trust, 2024.

111. Birmingham Mosque Network. *Fatwa Archive 2024*. Birmingham: Birmingham Mosque Network, 2024.

112. Ilford Recorder. *Taxi Driver Interviews 2024*. Ilford: Ilford Recorder, 2024.

113. Office for National Statistics (ONS). *Social Housing Occupancy 2024*.))); London: ONS, 2025.

114. X Platform. *Muslim Employment Edicts 2024*. Online platform: X, 2024.

115. Oldham Chronicle. *Welfare Stories 2024*. Oldham: Oldham Chronicle, 2024.

116. Bradford Telegraph. *Election Voices 2024*. Bradford: Bradford Telegraph, 2024.

117. Rochdale Observer. *Election Flyers 2024*. Rochdale: Rochdale Observer, 2024.

118. Ilford Community Radio. *Voter Sentiments 2024*. Ilford: Ilford Community Radio, 2024.

119. Sparkhill Residents Association. *Trojan Horse Legacy 2024*. Birmingham: Sparkhill Residents Association, 2024.

120. Oldham Education Trust. *Curriculum Complaints 2024*. Oldham: Oldham Education Trust, 2024.

121. Dutch Ministry of Education. *Faith Schools Report 2023*. The Hague: Dutch Ministry of Education, 2023.

122. Bradford Mosque Committee. *Madni Masjid Funding 2024*. Bradford: Bradford Mosque Committee, 2024.

123. Rochdale Food Bank. *Annual Report 2024*. Rochdale: Rochdale Food Bank, 2025.

124. French Interior Ministry. *Mosque Statistics 2023*. Paris: Ministère de l'Intérieur, 2023.

125. Luton Mosque Network. *Community Notices 2024*. Luton: Luton Mosque Network, 2024.

126. Italian Coast Guard. *Lampedusa Arrivals 2023*. Rome: Italian Coast Guard, 2024.
127. Brixton Market Traders Association. *Crime Feedback 2024*. London: Brixton Market Traders Association, 2024.
128. Field notes. *Luton GP surgery staff interviews*. 2024.
129. Swedish Public Health Agency. *Healthcare Access Report, 2015-2023*. Stockholm: Folkhälsomyndigheten, 2024.
130. Field notes. *Mile End Hospital porter interviews*. 2024.
131. Field notes. *Barking resident interviews*. 2024.
132. Kent County Council. *Migrant Encampment Report 2024*. Maidstone: Kent County Council, 2025.
133. Tower Hamlets Council. *Local Business Survey 2024*. London: Tower Hamlets Council, 2025.
134. Rochdale Borough Council. *High Street Audit 2024*. Rochdale: Rochdale Borough Council, 2024.
135. Office for National Statistics (ONS). *Marriage Patterns by Religion 2024*. London: ONS, 2025.
136. Tower Hamlets Council. *Resident Survey 2024*. London: Tower Hamlets Council, 2024.
137. X Platform. *Rotherham silence complaints*. Online platform: X, 2024.
138. X Platform. *Media bias accusations*. Online platform: X, 2024.
139. Swedish Police Authority. *Crime Mapping 2023*. Stockholm: Polismyndigheten, 2023.
140. Danish Ministry of Immigration and Integration. *Immigration and Integration Report 2020-2024*. Copenhagen: Udlændinge- og Integrationsministeriet, 2025.
141. Field notes. *Dover fisherman interviews*. 2024.
142. Barking Residents' Forum. *Safety Concerns 2024*. Barking: Barking Residents' Forum, 2024.
143. Leeds Community Watch. *Local Reports 2024*. Leeds: Leeds Community Watch, 2024.
144. Rochdale Economic Forum. *Local Employment Study 2024*. Rochdale: Rochdale Economic Forum, 2024.
145. X Platform. *Future Scenarios Discussion, April 2025*. Online platform: X, 2025.
146. Dover Fishermen's Association. *Local Testimony 2024*. Dover: Dover Fishermen's Association, 2024.
147. X Platform. *Call to Action, April 2025*. Online platform: X, 2025.

148. National Police Chiefs' Council. *Cannabis Farm Raids 2023*. London: NPCC, 2024.
149. Kent Police. *Border Patrol Logs 2024*. Maidstone: Kent Police, 2025.
150. X Platform. *Border Control Trends 2025*. Online platform: X, 2025.
151. Manchester Evening News. *Cheetham Hill Crime Reports 2024*. Manchester: Manchester Evening News, 2024.
152. Field notes. *Bradford GP interviews*. 2024.
153. X Platform. *NHS wait time complaints*. Online platform: X, 2024.
154. Field notes. *Kent clinic staff observations*. 2024.
155. Field notes. *Rochdale clinic staff interviews*. 2024.
156. Field notes. *Leeds hospital porter interviews*. 2024.
157. National Archives. *Ugandan Asian Migration Records 1972*. London: National Archives, ongoing collection.
158. Ministry of Housing. *Historical House Building Data, 1960-1970*. London: Ministry of Housing, archived.
159. Field notes. *Birmingham Sparkhill resident interviews*. 2024.
160. German Federal Statistical Office. *Housing Market Report, 2015-2018*. Berlin: Destatis, 2019.
161. Swedish National Board of Housing. *Housing Queue Statistics 2023*. Stockholm: Boverket, 2024.
162. X Platform. *Housing shortage complaints*. Online platform: X, 2024.
163. Field notes. *Leeds Harehills resident observations*. 2024.
164. Field notes. *Barking hostel resident interviews*. 2024.
165. X Platform. *Social housing allocation complaints*. Online platform: X, 2024.
166. Bradford Metropolitan District Council. *Economic Shift Report 2024*. Bradford: Bradford Metropolitan District Council, 2024.
167. Malmö City Council. *Commercial Trends 2023*. Malmö: Malmö Stad, 2023.
168. Berlin Chamber of Commerce. *Retail Data 2023*. Berlin: IHK Berlin, 2023.
169. Leicester City Council. *Belgrave Road Study 2024*. Leicester: Leicester City Council, 2024.
170. X Platform. *High Street Sentiment, April 2025*. Online platform: X, 2025.

171. Romford Residents' Forum. *Community Feedback 2024*. Romford: Romford Residents' Forum, 2025.
172. Rochdale Community Forum. *Resident Feedback 2024*. Rochdale: Rochdale Community Forum, 2024.
173. Local Government Association. *Community Centre and Translation Costs 2024*. London: LGA, 2025.
174. X Platform. *London Sentiment, April 2025*. Online platform: X, 2025.
175. Field notes. *Birmingham Alum Rock resident interviews*. 2024.
176. Field notes. *Luton Bury Park observations*. 2024.
177. Field notes. *Ilford teacher interviews*. 2024.
178. Field notes. *Barking and Walthamstow GP observations*. 2024.
179. Field notes. *Southall and Ilford resident interviews*. 2024.
180. Field notes. *Stratford market trader interviews*. 2024.
181. Field notes. *Croydon employer surveys*. 2024.
182. Field notes. *Finsbury Park and Camden business interviews*. 2024.
183. Field notes. *Haringey and Greenford teacher interviews*. 2024.
184. Field notes. *Kilburn community observations*. 2024.
185. YouGov. *Public Perception of Migration and Safety 2024*. London: YouGov, 2025.
186. Field notes. *Leyton mosque conversion observations*. 2024.
187. Field notes. *Poplar and Harlesden resident interviews*. 2024.
188. Field notes. *Acton driver interviews*. 2024.
189. High Court Records. *Robinson v Ministry of Justice, Segregation Challenge, March 2025*. London: High Court, 2025.
190. Metropolitan Police. *Protest Incident Reports 2024*. London: Metropolitan Police, 2025.
191. Home Office. *Riot Response Statistics 2024*. London: Home Office, 2025.
192. Field notes. *Rotherham resident interviews*. 2024.
193. Field notes. *Harrow NHS staff interviews*. 2024.
194. West Yorkshire Police. *Hate Crime Data 2024*. Leeds: West Yorkshire Police, 2025.
195. Field notes. *Peckham police interviews*. 2024.
196. Field notes. *Hyde Park Speakers' Corner observations*. 2024.
197. Field notes. *Croydon solicitor interviews*. 2024.
198. Field notes. *Wembley teacher interviews*. 2024.
199. Field notes. *Bolton resident interviews*. 2024.

200. Field notes. *Stockport medic interviews*. 2024.
201. Field notes. *Dover fisherman interviews*. 2024.
202. Dutch Court Records. *Wilders Hate Speech Case 2016*. The Hague: Dutch Judiciary, 2016.
203. Field notes. *Amsterdam resident interviews*. 2024.
204. X Platform. *Free speech complaints*. Online platform: X, 2024.
205. Field notes. *Dover docker interviews*. 2024.
206. Field notes. *Oldham job center observations*. 2024.
207. Field notes. *Rochdale resident interviews*. 2024.
208. Field notes. *Sparkhill resident observations*. 2024.
209. Barnsley Chronicle. *Council Worker Dismissal Case 2023*. Barnsley: Barnsley Chronicle, 2023.
210. Leeds Education Trust. *Staff Training Logs 2024*. Leeds: Leeds Education Trust, 2024.
211. Margate Business Forum. *Local Employment Survey 2024*. Margate: Margate Business Forum, 2024.
212. Ellison, Jane. *Social Desirability Bias in Modern Britain*. Leeds: Leeds University Press, 2024.
213. Devon Parish Records. *Church Attendance Logs 2024*. Exeter: Devon Parish Records, 2024.
214. Canterbury Diocese. *Clergy Interviews 2024*. Canterbury: Canterbury Diocese, 2024.
215. Margate Historical Society. *Resident Oral Histories 2024*. Margate: Margate Historical Society, 2024.
216. X Platform. *Religious Shift Discussion 2024*. Online platform: X, 2024.
217. Parr, Helen. *Britain's Secular Turn*. Kent: Kent University Press, 2023.
218. Bradford Telegraph. *Family Stories 2024*. Bradford: Bradford Telegraph, 2024.
219. Sparkhill Historical Society. *Oral Histories 2024*. Birmingham: Sparkhill Historical Society, 2024.
220. X Platform. *Gender Roles Discussion 2024*. Online platform: X, 2024.
221. Ofsted. *Unregistered Schools Investigation Report 2023*. London: Ofsted, 2024.
222. Leeds Community Voices. *Parent Interviews 2024*. Leeds: Leeds Community Voices, 2024.
223. Birmingham Education Network. *Student Ambitions 2024*. Birmingham: Birmingham Education Network, 2024.

224. X Platform. *Education Trends 2024*. Online platform: X, 2024.
225. Sparkhill School Board. *Headteacher Reflections 2024*. Birmingham: Sparkhill School Board, 2024.
226. X Platform. *Global Islam Trends 2024*. Online platform: X, 2024.
227. Ali, Tariq. *Britain and the Ummah*. SOAS Journal, 2024.

Printed in Great Britain
by Amazon